HYPER KETOSIS DIET FOOD LIST

Essential Guide to Delicious & Tasty Low-Carb Recipes Including Shopping Lists, and a 30-Day Plan for Optimal Weight Loss

Dr. Laurel Neel

Disclaimer

The information contained in this book is for educational and informational purposes only and is not intended as health or medical advice. The author and publisher are not responsible for any specific health or allergy needs that may require medical supervision and are not liable for any damages or negative consequences from any treatment, action, application, or preparation to any person reading or following the information in this book. References are provided for informational purposes only and do not constitute an endorsement of any websites or other sources.

TABLE OF CONTENTS

Chapter 1. Introduction to Hyper Ketosis

In the quiet corners of our family's kitchen, a new chapter began for my loved one, Linda. Her journey with hyper ketosis started not out of choice but necessity—a response to an unrelenting wave of health challenges that traditional methods couldn't seem to conquer. I remember vividly the day Linda sat across from me, her face a mix of determination and frustration, as she wrestled with the implications of her latest blood work. Her doctor had recommended a drastic change: a hyper ketosis diet.

At first, the concept seemed daunting. The strict parameters of the hyper ketosis diet—extremely low carbohydrates, high fats, and moderate proteins—felt like a far cry from the meals we had grown accustomed to. Yet, Linda's resolve was unshakeable. She was ready to embark on this uncharted journey for the sake of her health.

The transition was anything but smooth. Linda began by swapping out her daily staples for keto-friendly alternatives—avocado for toast, cauliflower for rice, and almond flour for breadcrumbs. She meticulously tracked her macronutrient intake, ensuring her body stayed within the ketosis threshold. The first few weeks were marked by challenges: cravings, fatigue, and a profound learning curve about the nuances of this diet.

But Linda was no stranger to perseverance. Gradually, the fog of initial discomfort lifted, revealing a new reality. Her energy levels soared, a surprising contrast to the sluggishness she had previously felt. The scales tipped in her favor as her weight began to normalize, and her blood glucose levels stabilized. Each day brought a sense of accomplishment, not just from the tangible health improvements but from mastering a diet that once seemed overwhelming.

Linda's kitchen transformed into a hub of creativity and resilience. We experimented with new recipes—zucchini noodles with creamy sauces, savory cauliflower crust pizzas, and rich, hearty stews. The hyper ketosis diet had become more than a regimen; it was a culinary adventure that redefined our understanding of food.

The benefits were profound. Linda's blood work improved dramatically, and her overall well-being was restored. The diet provided her with a renewed sense of vitality and control over her health. It was a testament to how a carefully managed diet could make a significant difference in one's life.

Her journey with the hyper ketosis diet was not just about adherence to a set of nutritional guidelines but about reclaiming her health and embracing a new way of living. As I share this story in the introduction of this book, I hope it serves as a beacon of hope for those embarking on their own journey. Linda's experience illustrates that with dedication, adaptability, and the right guidance, even the most challenging dietary transformations can lead to remarkable outcomes.

In the chapters that follow, you will find a collection of recipes and insights designed to make the hyper ketosis diet accessible and enjoyable. Each dish reflects Linda's journey—a testament to the vibrant possibilities that this diet can offer.

Understanding Ketosis: The metabolic state of fat-burning

Having a solid understanding of the core notion of ketosis itself is absolutely necessary before delving into the intricacies of hyper ketosis. In essence, ketosis is a normal metabolic state when your body converts its primary fuel source from glucose (derived from carbohydrates) to ketones (derived from fat).

In general, glucose is the primary source of energy for your body. The condition of ketosis, on the other hand, is induced in your body when you dramatically cut back on the amount of carbohydrates you consume. When you are in this state, your liver begins to convert fatty acids into ketones. Ketones provide your brain, muscles, and other organs with the primary source of fuel that they need to function properly.

Your body will undergo a number of major changes as a result of this metabolic shift. First and foremost, it encourages the burning of fat, which makes it an appealing choice for individuals who are looking to reduce their body fat percentage or enhance their body composition. Ketosis has also been linked to a number of additional advantages, including an increase in energy levels, an improvement in mental clarity, a reduction in inflammation, and even the possibility of therapeutic effects for a number of medical diseases.

Taking ketosis to the next level is what hyperketosis is all about.

While ketosis itself offers a range of benefits, hyper ketosis takes it a step further. It is a state of increased ketosis when your blood ketone levels are much higher than in typical ketosis. This is often done through a combination of very low carbohydrate intake, increased fat consumption, and sometimes the use of exogenous ketones (ketone supplements).

Hyper ketosis is commonly sought after by persons wanting to optimize the benefits of a ketogenic diet. The higher ketone levels can lead to even greater fat burning, enhanced cognitive function, and improved physical performance. Additionally, some research suggests that hyper ketosis may have significant therapeutic benefits, notably in areas such as epilepsy and certain neurological illnesses.

Benefits and Risks: Weighing the Pros and Cons

As with every dietary plan, hyper ketosis has its own set of potential benefits and risks. It is critical to weigh them thoroughly before embarking on this quest.

Potential Benefits:

1. **Accelerated Fat Burning:** Hyper ketosis can greatly enhance your body's fat-burning capacity, resulting in weight loss and enhancing body composition.
2. **Enhanced Cognitive Function:** The brain thrives on ketones, and higher ketone levels may lead to improved focus, mental clarity, and general cognitive function.
3. **Increased Energy Levels:** Many people report feeling more invigorated and less weary when in a condition of hyper ketosis.
4. **Improved Athletic Performance:** Some athletes find that hyper ketosis helps them sustain energy levels and perform better during endurance activities.
5. **Potential Therapeutic Applications:** Research suggests that hyper ketosis may be advantageous for managing some medical disorders, such as epilepsy, Alzheimer's disease, and certain types of cancer.

Potential Risks:

1. **Nutrient Deficiencies:** Strict carbohydrate restriction can make it tough to achieve all your nutritional demands. Careful planning and supplements may be necessary.
2. **Electrolyte Imbalance:** Increased urine and changes in mineral excretion can lead to electrolyte imbalances, potentially producing symptoms including muscle cramps, weariness, and headaches.
3. **The "Keto Flu":** As your body learns to use ketones for fuel, you may experience transient side effects like fatigue, headache, nausea, and irritability.
4. **Social Challenges:** Adhering to a hyper ketosis diet can be tough in social contexts and may require extra planning and preparation.
5. **Potential Long-Term Risks:** The long-term implications of hyper ketosis are not well recognized. It's vital to check with a healthcare practitioner before commencing on this technique, especially if you have any underlying health concerns.

Chapter 2: Principle of Hyper Ketosis Diet and Nutritional Guidelines

The hyper ketosis diet is an advanced approach within the ketogenic diet framework, aimed at producing and maintaining a state of ketosis at a deeper and more prolonged level. This strategy is typically adopted by persons seeking greater fat loss, improved mental clarity, and optimized metabolic efficiency. Here's an in-depth look at the principles and dietary criteria of the hyper ketosis diet:

Principle of Hyper Ketosis Diet

1. Enhanced Ketosis:

Objective: Achieve a more profound state of ketosis compared to regular ketogenic diets. Hyper ketosis tries to greatly boost ketone levels in the blood, often reaching levels that are higher than those generally found on a standard keto diet.

Mechanism: This is accomplished by a stricter macronutrient ratio and additional tactics to force the body into deeper ketosis. The primary focus is on very low carbohydrate intake mixed with moderate protein and substantial fat consumption.

2. Low Carbohydrate Intake:

Goal: Keep carbohydrate consumption extremely low to reduce glucose availability, so forcing the body to rely more heavily on ketones for energy.

Typical Range: Carbohydrate intake is generally lowered to fewer than 20 grams per day, which is below the range usually suggested in standard ketogenic diets.

3. Moderate Protein Consumption:

Balance: Protein intake is controlled to ensure that it is sufficient for muscle maintenance and repair without exceeding levels that could potentially be turned into glucose (gluconeogenesis).

Typical Range: Protein intake generally falls between 0.6 to 1.0 grams per kilogram of body weight per day, depending on individual needs and goals.

4. High Fat Intake:

Primary Energy Source: The majority of calories come from fats, which are used to make ketones and give energy.

Typical Range: Fat consumption can constitute 70-80% of daily calories, ensuring that there is adequate fat available to support persistent ketosis.

5. Consistent Ketone Monitoring:

Tracking: Regular monitoring of ketone levels using blood, urine, or breath tests to ensure that ketosis is being maintained and modified as needed.

Objective: Achieve and maintain increased amounts of ketones (typically above 1.5 mmol/L in blood tests) to ensure profound ketosis.

6. Potential Use of Supplements:

Ketone Supplements: Some persons use exogenous ketones to support and accelerate the state of ketosis, especially during the early adaption phase or to reach greater ketone levels.

7. Emphasis on Whole Foods:

Nutrient-Dense: Focus on consuming nutrient-dense, whole foods to guarantee adequate intake of vitamins and minerals, despite the restrictive character of the diet.

Nutritional Guidelines for Hyper Ketosis Diet

1. Carbohydrates:

Sources: Limit to non-starchy veggies (e.g., leafy greens, cruciferous vegetables), modest servings of berries, and occasionally low-carb fruits.

Amount: Aim for less than 20 grams of net carbs per day (total carbs minus fiber).

2. Protein:

Sources: Include moderate amounts of protein from animal sources (meat, chicken, fish) and plant-based options (tofu, tempeh).

Amount: Typically, 0.6 to 1.0 grams per kilogram of body weight each day. Adjust based on activity levels and specific goals.

3. Fats:

Sources: Focus on healthy fats such as avocados, nuts, seeds, olive oil, coconut oil, and fatty seafood. Include saturated fats (from animal sources) and monounsaturated fats for balance.

Amount: Approximately 70-80% of total daily calories.

4. Hydration and Electrolytes:

Importance: Maintain appropriate hydration and electrolyte balance to support metabolic activities and prevent symptoms of the "keto flu."

Recommendations: Drink plenty of water and consider supplementing with electrolytes (sodium, potassium, magnesium) as needed.

5. Meal Timing and Frequency:

Intermittent Fasting: Some individuals combine hyper ketosis with intermittent fasting to boost ketone generation and metabolic efficiency.

Eating Windows: Typical fasting times can range from 16 hours fast with an 8-hour eating window (16/8) to lengthier fasting periods, depending on individual tolerance and goals.

6. Avoiding High Glycemic Foods:

Foods to Avoid: Steer clear of high-glycemic index foods, including sweets, refined grains, and starchy vegetables, which can boost blood glucose levels and interfere with ketosis.

7. Monitoring and Adjusting:

Regular Testing: Regularly test blood ketone levels and adjust food intake as needed to maintain target ketone levels.

Adaptation Phase: Be conscious of the adaptation period where the body adjusts to burning ketones for energy. This period can span several weeks.

The hyper ketosis diet is designed for those wishing to establish and prolong a deep state of ketosis for specific metabolic or health goals. It involves careful planning and monitoring to ensure that the diet remains successful and wholesome.

Foods to Avoid on a Hyper Ketosis Diet

Maintaining a state of hyper ketosis necessitates careful adherence to an extremely low-carbohydrate diet. While this may seem difficult at first, recognizing which meals to avoid is vital for success. By avoiding clear of these high-carb culprits, you can ensure your body remains in fat-burning mode and reap the full benefits of this metabolic state.

Let's go more into the foods you should avoid on a hyper ketosis diet:

1. Grains and Starches:

Bread, pasta, rice, and cereals: These are strong in carbohydrates and will quickly boost your blood sugar levels, limiting ketone generation.

Baked products and pastries: Cakes, cookies, muffins, and doughnuts are filled with sugar and refined flour, which are big hurdles to ketosis.

Legumes: Beans, lentils, and peas, while nutritious, contain a substantial quantity of carbs and should be reduced or avoided on a high ketosis diet.

Starchy veggies: Potatoes, corn, and sweet potatoes are higher in carbohydrates compared to other vegetables and should be consumed sparingly or avoided altogether.

2. Sugary Drinks and Foods:

Soda, fruit juice, and sports drinks: These are filled with sugar and will boost your blood sugar levels, interrupting ketosis.

Candy, chocolate, and ice cream: These sugary indulgences are heavy in carbs and can easily derail your progress.

Sweetened condiments: Ketchup, barbecue sauce, and sweetened salad dressings often include hidden sugars, so check labels carefully or choose for unsweetened alternatives.

3. High-Carb Fruits:

Bananas, grapes, and mangoes: While fruits are generally healthful, some varieties are heavier in carbohydrates than others. Limit or avoid these fruits on a hyper ketosis diet.

Dried fruits: Dried fruits are high in sugar and should be avoided as they can quickly contribute to surpassing your daily carb allowance.

4. Alcohol:

Beer, wine, and cocktails: Alcohol is processed differently in a state of ketosis and can interfere with ketone synthesis. It's better to avoid alcohol or consume it in moderation, opting for low-carb options like dry wine or spirits with sugar-free mixers.

5. Processed Foods:

Packaged snacks and convenience foods: These are generally heavy in harmful fats, processed carbs, and added sugars, making them inappropriate for a hyper ketosis diet.

Processed foods: While meat is a necessity on a keto diet, processed kinds like hot dogs, sausages, and deli meats can include hidden sugars and fillers, so prefer fresh, unprocessed meats wherever possible.

6. Hidden Sources of Carbs:

Certain condiments and sauces: Some condiments and sauces, such as ketchup and barbecue sauce, might contain hidden sugars. Be cautious to read labels carefully or choose unsweetened alternatives.

Drugs and supplements: Some drugs and supplements may include hidden sugars or fillers. Consult your healthcare practitioner or pharmacist to check they are suitable for your hyper ketosis diet.

Chapter 3. Essential Fats for Hyper Ketosis

Healthy Fats: The Cornerstone of Your Diet

When it comes to achieving and living in a state of hyper ketosis, lipids are not merely a dietary component; they're the essential foundation upon which this metabolic state is based. Unlike traditional diets that sometimes condemn fats, a hyper ketosis diet embraces them as the major source of fuel, providing the energy your body needs to function optimally while boosting fat burning and other health advantages.

Understanding the Importance of Fats

In a hyper ketosis state, your body moves from depending on glucose from carbohydrates to utilizing ketones obtained from fat. This metabolic change needs a large increase in dietary fat intake, often about 70-80% of your total daily calories. By emphasizing healthy fats, you give your body the required building blocks to make ketones efficiently, powering your brain, muscles, and other organs.

Choosing the Right Fats

Not all fats are created equal. While a hyper ketosis diet allows for a higher fat intake, it's vital to focus on healthy fats that support general health and well-being. These include:

1. **Monounsaturated Fats:** Found in foods like avocados, olive oil, almonds, and seeds, these fats can help enhance heart health, reduce inflammation, and promote healthy cholesterol levels.
2. **Polyunsaturated Fats:** Sources include fatty fish (salmon, mackerel, sardines), flaxseeds, chia seeds, and walnuts contain vital omega-3 fatty acids, which are crucial for brain health, cardiovascular function, and immune system support.
3. **Saturated Fats:** While often demonized, moderate amounts of saturated fats from sources like coconut oil, grass-fed butter, and full-fat dairy can be consumed in a hyper ketosis diet. They provide a stable source of energy and assist hormone production.
4. **Avoiding Unhealthy Fats**
5. While fats are vital, it's important to avoid bad fats that might severely affect your health. These include:
6. **Trans Fats:** Found in processed foods and some margarine, trans fats are chemically manufactured and have been linked to increased heart disease risk, inflammation, and other health concerns.
7. **Highly Processed Vegetable Oils:** Oils like soybean oil, corn oil, and canola oil are generally highly processed and can contain dangerous levels of omega-6 fatty acids, which can contribute to inflammation.

MCT Oil: A Quick Source of Ketones

Medium-chain triglycerides (MCTs) are a unique type of fat that can be particularly advantageous for persons following a hyper ketosis diet. Unlike long-chain fatty acids found in most dietary lipids, MCTs are swiftly absorbed and delivered directly to the liver, where they are promptly transformed into ketones. This makes MCT oil a helpful tool for raising ketone levels and providing a quickly available source of energy.

Benefits of MCT Oil:

- **Rapid Ketone Production:** MCT oil can help you attain and sustain a state of ketosis more quickly, especially when shifting to a hyper ketosis diet.
- **Increased Energy and Focus:** The rapid conversion of MCTs into ketones can provide an immediate energy boost and improve mental clarity.
- **Appetite Suppression:** MCT oil may help reduce appetite and enhance feelings of fullness, aiding in weight management.
- **Improved Gut Health:** MCTs have antibacterial characteristics and may help sustain a healthy gut microbiota.

Incorporating MCT Oil into Your Diet:

MCT oil can be readily added to smoothies, coffee, and salad dressings, or even taken on its own. Start with modest doses and gradually increase your intake to test your tolerance.

Avocados: Creamy and Packed with Nutrients

Avocados have developed a well-deserved reputation as a nutritional powerhouse, and they truly shine in a high ketosis diet. Their creamy texture and mild flavor make them flexible food, while their outstanding nutritional profile offers a myriad of benefits for individuals following this dietary approach.

Key Benefits:

- **High in Healthy Fats:** Avocados are largely composed of monounsaturated fats, notably oleic acid, which has been linked to enhanced heart health, lower inflammation, and better blood sugar control. These fats are vital for fueling your body in ketosis and encouraging fat burning.
- **Rich in Fiber:** Avocados are a wonderful source of dietary fiber, which aids in digestion, maintains gut health, and adds to feelings of fullness and satisfaction. This can be particularly helpful when following a limited diet like hyper ketosis.
- **Nutrient-Dense:** Avocados are filled with critical vitamins and minerals, including potassium, magnesium, vitamin K, vitamin E, and B vitamins. These nutrients support

different body functions, including muscular contraction, neuron function, blood coagulation, and energy production.

Ways to Incorporate Avocados into Your Hyper Ketosis Diet:

- **Sliced or mashed on salads:** Add a creamy and nutritious ingredient to your salads.
- **Blended into smoothies:** Create a rich and delicious smoothie foundation.
- **Guacamole:** A classic keto-friendly dip ideal for vegetables or low-carb crackers.
- **Avocado toast (with keto-friendly bread):** A satisfying breakfast or snack choice.
- **Stuffed avocados:** Fill avocado halves with a variety of keto-friendly toppings for a quick and easy lunch.

Fatty Fish: Omega-3s for Heart Health

Fatty fish, such as salmon, mackerel, sardines, and herring, are a great addition to a hyper ketosis diet due to their high omega-3 fatty acid concentration. These necessary fats offer several benefits for overall health, notably for heart health and brain function.

Key Benefits:

- **Rich in Omega-3s:** Omega-3 fatty acids, particularly EPA and DHA, have been found to reduce inflammation, promote heart health, lower blood pressure, and support healthy cholesterol levels. These benefits are vital for anyone following a hyper ketosis diet, as it emphasizes fat intake.
- **Excellent Source of , Protein:** Fatty fish delivers a good amount of high-quality protein, which is vital for growing and maintaining muscle mass, promoting satiety, and aiding in numerous biological activities.
- **Nutrient-Dense:** Fatty fish also contains critical vitamins and minerals, including vitamin D, B vitamins, selenium, and potassium, which help to overall health and well-being.

Ways to Incorporate Fatty Fish into Your Hyper Ketosis Diet:

- **Grilled or baked:** A simple and delightful way to enjoy fatty fish.
- **Pan-seared:** Creates a crispy skin and delicious flesh.
- **Added to salads:** Flaked salmon or tuna can provide protein and healthy fats to your salads.
- **Salmon patties:** A delicious and practical way to add more salmon to your diet.
- **Fish soup or stew:** A pleasant and healthful meal option.
- **Nuts and Seeds:** Convenient Snacks for Hyper Ketosis

In the domain of hyper ketosis, where dietary discipline is crucial, having a stash of quick and keto-friendly snacks can be a lifesaver. Nuts and seeds emerge as champions in this area, giving a great combination of crunch, flavor, and critical nutrients that perfectly complement this high-fat, low-carb lifestyle.

Why Nuts and Seeds are Ideal for Hyper Ketosis:

1. **High in Healthy Fats:** Nuts and seeds are abundant in healthy fats, mostly monounsaturated and polyunsaturated fats, which are vital for feeding your body in ketosis and maintaining general health. These fats help you feel full, give prolonged energy, and support numerous biological functions.
2. **Good Source of , Protein:** While not as protein-rich as animal sources, nuts and seeds deliver a reasonable quantity of plant-based protein, helping with muscle maintenance and repair, satiety, and overall well-being.
3. **Rich in Fiber:** Fiber plays a critical function in digestive health, blood sugar regulation, and promoting a sensation of fullness. Nuts and seeds offer a decent dose of fiber, helping you keep on track with your hyper ketosis goals.
4. **Nutrient Powerhouses:** Nuts and seeds are filled with critical vitamins and minerals, including magnesium, potassium, vitamin E, and selenium. These nutrients serve vital roles in different biological activities, supporting everything from bone health to immunological function.
5. **Convenient and Portable:** Nuts and seeds are inherently portable and require no preparation, making them excellent for on-the-go snacking or adding to meals and recipes.

Top Picks for Hyper Ketosis:

Almonds: A popular and adaptable choice, almonds are rich in vitamin E, magnesium, and fiber.

Walnuts: These brain-shaped nuts are filled with omega-3 fatty acids, known for their heart-healthy and cognitive benefits.

Macadamia Nuts: Boasting the highest fat content among nuts, macadamia nuts are a keto dieter's dream, giving a rich, buttery flavor.

Pecans: With a somewhat sweet taste, pecans are a good source of antioxidants and healthy fats.

Brazil Nuts: Just a few Brazil nuts deliver a large amount of selenium, a critical element for thyroid health and immunological function.

Chia Seeds: These tiny seeds are filled with fiber, omega-3s, and protein, making them a fantastic addition to smoothies, yogurt, or chia pudding.

Flaxseeds: Another good source of omega-3s and fiber, flaxseeds can be crushed and added to various foods for a nutritional boost.

Pumpkin Seeds: These tasty seeds are rich in magnesium, zinc, and antioxidants.

Incorporating Nuts and Seeds into Your Diet:

- **Snacking:** Enjoy a handful of nuts or seeds as a quick and tasty snack between meals.
- Salads and Bowls: Sprinkle nuts and seeds over salads or grain-free bowls for extra crunch, taste, and minerals.
- **Homemade Trail Mix:** Create your own keto-friendly trail mix by blending nuts, seeds, unsweetened coconut flakes, and dark chocolate chips.
- **Nut Butter:** Choose natural nut butter without added sugar or oils for a wonderful spread on keto-friendly bread or vegetables.
- **Seed Crackers:** Make your own low-carb crackers with ground flaxseeds or chia seeds.

A Word of Caution:

While nuts and seeds are healthful and useful, they are also calorie-dense. It's crucial to practice portion control and be cautious of your overall calorie intake, especially while striving for hyper ketosis.

Chapter 4. Breakfast

Bulletproof Coffee

Bulletproof coffee is the cornerstone of many ketogenic diets. The mix of healthy fats from butter and MCT oil gives sustained energy, suppresses appetite, and boosts mental clarity, making it a great way to start your day in hyper ketosis.

Prep Time: 5 minutes | Cooking Time: 0 minutes | Total Time: 5 minutes | Serving Size: 1

Ingredients:

- 1 cup freshly brewed coffee (ideally organic)
- 1-2 tablespoons unsalted grass-fed butter or ghee
- 1-2 tablespoons MCT oil

Method of Preparation:

1. Brew your coffee as you normally would.
2. Add the butter and MCT oil to the hot coffee.
3. Blend with an immersion blender or with a standard blender until smooth and frothy.
4. Pour into your favorite cup and enjoy!

Nutritional Value (Approximate):

Calories: 200-300, Fat: 20-30g, Protein: 0-1g, Carbs: 0-1g

Note: Adjust the amount of butter and MCT oil to your particular preference and nutritional needs. You can also add a pinch of cinnamon or other keto-friendly spices for taste.

Avocado with Smoked Salmon Toast

This exquisite breakfast option mixes the creamy richness of avocado with the smoky flavor of salmon, offering a gratifying dose of healthy fats and protein to fuel your hyper ketosis journey. The Everything But the Bagel spice adds a savory touch, giving this a genuinely gourmet keto breakfast.

Prep Time: 10 minutes | Cooking Time: 0 minutes | Total Time: 10 minutes | Serving Size: 1

Ingredients:

1. 1 slice keto-friendly bread or 2-3 keto crackers
2. 1/2 ripe avocado, mashed
3. 2-3 ounces smoked salmon
4. 1/4 lemon, for squeezing
5. Everything But the Bagel spice, to taste

Method of Preparation:

1. Toast the keto bread or crackers lightly.
2. Spread the mashed avocado equally over the toast or crackers.
3. Top with smoked salmon slices.
4. Squeeze fresh lemon juice over the salmon.

5. Sprinkle with Everything But the Bagel seasoning.
6. Enjoy immediately!

Nutritional Value (Approximate):

Calories: 300-400, Fat: 25-35g, Protein: 15-20g, Carbs: 5-8g

Note: Choose a keto-friendly bread or cracker with minimum carbohydrates. You can also experiment with alternative toppings, such as sliced cucumber, red onion, or capers.

Keto Pancakes

Indulge in a plate of fluffy pancakes without jeopardizing your hyper ketosis goals. These keto pancakes, made with almond and coconut flour, are a tasty and gratifying way to start your day. Top them with fresh berries and sugar-free syrup for a guilt-free delight.

Prep Time: 10 minutes | Cooking Time: 15 minutes | Total Time: 25 minutes | Serving Size: 2-3

Ingredients:

- 1/2 cup almond flour
- 1/4 cup coconut flour
- 2 big eggs
- 1/4 cup unsweetened almond or coconut milk
- 1/4 teaspoon baking powder
- 1/4 teaspoon salt
- 1/4 teaspoon vanilla extract
- 1-2 teaspoons sweetener of choice (e.g., stevia, monk fruit)
- Butter or coconut oil, for coating the pan
- Fresh berries with sugar-free syrup, for serving

Method of Preparation:

1. Mix the coconut flour, almond flour, baking powder, and salt in a bigger basin.
2. In a separate bowl, whisk together the eggs, almond/coconut milk, vanilla extract, and sweetener.
3. After adding the wet components to the dry ingredients, whisk just enough to combine them. Avoid overmixing.
4. Heat a skillet or griddle over medium heat and grease lightly with butter or coconut oil.
5. Pour 1/4 cup of batter into the heated pan for each pancake.
6. Cook for 2-3 minutes per side, or until golden brown and heated through.
7. Serve with fresh berries and sugar-free syrup.

Nutritional Value (Per Serving):

Calories: 200-250, Fat: 15-20g, Protein: 8-10g, Carbs: 5-7g

Note: You can modify the sweetness and flavor of the pancakes by adding different spices or extracts. Experiment with toppings like whipped cream, almonds, or seeds for more variety.

Bacon with Eggs

A classic breakfast combination that is naturally keto-friendly, bacon and eggs offer a hearty and delicious start to your day. The protein and fat in this meal will keep you feeling full and energized for hours, making it a perfect choice for individuals following a hyper ketosis diet.

Prep Time: 5 minutes | Cooking Time: 10-15 minutes | Total Time: 15-20 minutes | Serving Size: 1

Ingredients:

- 3-4 slices bacon
- 2-3 big eggs
- Salt and pepper to taste

Method of Preparation:

1. Fry the bacon in a skillet over medium heat until it becomes crispy. Take out the bacon from the skillet and set it aside to drain on a dish covered with paper towels.
2. In the same skillet, crack the eggs and fry to your desired level of doneness (scrambled, fried, or sunny-side up). Season with salt and pepper.
3. Serve the bacon and eggs together and enjoy!

Nutritional Value (Approximate):

Calories: 350-450, Fat: 30-40g, Protein: 20-25g, Carbs: 1-2g

Note: You can add diversity to this classic recipe by mixing alternative cooking methods or adding keto-friendly vegetables like spinach, mushrooms, or bell peppers to your scrambled eggs.

Chia Pudding

Chia pudding is a versatile and healthful breakfast that is excellent for meal prep. Its creamy texture and customizable tastes make it a great way to start your day. Chia seeds provide you with protein, fiber, and omega-3 fatty acids to keep you full and energized all morning long.

Prep Time: 10 minutes | Cooking Time: 0 minutes (needs refrigerator overnight) | Total Time: 10 minutes prep + overnight refrigeration | Serving Size: 1

Ingredients:

- ¼ cup chia seeds
- One cup of unsweetened almond milk (or another keto-friendly milk option)
- 1-2 teaspoons sweetener of choice (e.g., stevia, monk fruit)
- ½ teaspoon vanilla extract (or additional flavorings like cocoa powder, or cinnamon)
- Berries and nuts, for topping

Method of Preparation:

1. Mix the chia seeds, almond milk, sweetener, and vanilla extract in a bowl or container.
2. Stir carefully to ensure the chia seeds are uniformly dispersed.
3. Cover and refrigerate overnight or for at least 4 hours, allowing the chia

seeds to absorb the liquid and develop a pudding-like consistency.

4. In the morning, top with your favorite fruit and nuts and enjoy!

Nutritional Value (Approximate):

Calories: 300-400, Fat: 25-30g, Protein: 10-12g, Carbs: 10-15g (depending on toppings)

Keto Breakfast Casserole

This rich and comforting casserole is excellent for meal prep and ensures you have a wonderful keto-friendly breakfast ready to go throughout the week. Packed with protein, healthy fats, and vegetables, it is a balanced meal to fuel your busy mornings.

Prep Time: 15 minutes | Cooking Time: 30-40 minutes | Total Time: 45-55 minutes | Serving Size: 4-6

Ingredients:

- 1 pound sausage, cooked and crumbled
- 6 big eggs
- One cup of shredded cheese (cheddar, mozzarella, or a mix)
- 1 cup chopped veggies (spinach, mushrooms, bell peppers, onions)
- Salt and pepper to taste

Method of Preparation:

1. Preheat oven to 350°F (175°C).
2. Whisk the eggs, salt, and pepper in a sizable basin.
3. Add cheese, chopped vegetables, and cooked sausage and stir.
4. Transfer mixture to a 9 x 13-inch baking dish that has been buttered.
5. Bake for 30 to 40 minutes, until the top of the casserole is golden brown and firm.
6. Allow it cool somewhat before slicing and serving.

Nutritional Value (Per Serving):

Calories: 300-350, Fat: 25-30g, Protein: 20-25g, Carbs: 3-5g

Keto Smoothie

This nutritious and low-fat keto smoothie is a simple and quick breakfast substitute. It's perfect for hectic mornings when you need a quick meal to keep you energized and concentrated.

Prep Time: 5 minutes | Cooking Time: 0 minutes | Total Time: 5 minutes | Serving Size: 1

Ingredients:

- 1 cup unsweetened almond or coconut milk
- 1 bunch spinach or kale
- ½ avocado
- 1 scoop protein powder (unflavored or vanilla)
- 1 tablespoon MCT oil
- ½ cup berries (strawberries, raspberries, blueberries)
- Ice cubes (optional)

Method of Preparation:

1. In a blender, add all ingredients and process until smooth.
2. If needed, add ice cubes and blend again until desired consistency is obtained.
3. Pour into a glass and enjoy immediately.

Nutritional Value (Approximate):

Calories: 350-400, Fat: 25-30g, Protein: 20-25g, Carbs: 10-12g

Keto Omelet

A keto omelet is a versatile and fulfilling breakfast choice that can be tailored to your liking. Packed with protein and healthy fats, it is a terrific way to start your day on a hyper ketosis diet.

Prep Time: 5 minutes | Cooking Time: 10 minutes | Total Time: 15 minutes | Serving Size: 1

Ingredients:

- 2-3 big eggs
- 1 tablespoon butter or olive oil
- ¼ cup shredded cheese (cheddar, mozzarella, or a mix)
- ½ cup chopped veggies (spinach, mushrooms, bell peppers, onions)
- Salt and pepper to taste

Method of Preparation:

1. In a small bowl, mix together eggs, salt, and pepper.
2. Heat butter or olive oil in a non-stick skillet over medium heat.
3. Pour the egg mixture into the skillet and let it cook for a minute or two, or until the edges start to solidify.
4. Sprinkle cheese and chopped vegetables over half of the omelet.
5. Carefully fold the omelet in half and cook for another minute or two, or until the cheese is melted and the vegetables are cooked through.
6. Slide the omelet onto a dish and serve immediately.

Nutritional Value (Approximate):

Calories: 300-350, Fat: 25-30g, Protein: 20-25g, Carbs: 3-5g

Bulletproof Matcha Latte

For a new and invigorating spin on the typical bulletproof coffee, try this Bulletproof Matcha Latte. Matcha delivers a lasting energy boost and antioxidants, while the healthy fats from butter and MCT oil promote satiety and mental clarity.

Prep Time: 5 minutes | Cooking Time: 0 minutes | Total Time: 5 minutes | Serving Size: 1

Ingredients:

- 1 cup hot water
- 1 teaspoon matcha powder
- 1-2 tablespoons unsalted grass-fed butter or ghee
- 1-2 tablespoons MCT oil

Method of Preparation:

1. Whisk matcha powder with hot water until smooth and frothy.
2. Pour MCT oil and butter into the matcha latte.
3. Blend with an immersion blender or with a normal blender until smooth and creamy
4. Pour into your favorite cup and enjoy

Nutritional Value (Approximate):

Calories: 200-300, Fat: 20-30g, Protein 0-1g, Carbs: 0-1g

Note: Adjust the amount of butter and MCT oil to your liking and dietary needs. You may also add a pinch of cinnamon or other keto-friendly spices for added flavor

Keto Yogurt Parfait

A keto yogurt parfait is a refreshing and visually appealing breakfast that mixes the creamy smoothness of Greek yogurt with the sweetness of berries and the crunch of nuts and seeds. It is a wonderful blend of protein, healthy fats, and fiber to keep you pleased and energized throughout the morning.

Prep Time: 5 minutes | Cooking Time: 0 minutes | Total Time: 5 minutes | Serving Size: 1

Ingredients:

- 1 cup unsweetened full-fat Greek yogurt
- ½ cup mixed berries (strawberries, raspberries, blueberries)
- ¼ cup chopped nuts (almonds, walnuts, pecans)
- 1 tablespoon chia seeds or flaxseeds
- 1 tablespoon unsweetened coconut flakes

Method of Preparation:

1. In a glass or dish, layer the Greek yogurt, berries, almonds, seeds, and coconut flakes.
2. Repeat the layers until all ingredients are utilized, concluding with a sprinkle of coconut flakes on top.
3. Enjoy immediately!

Nutritional Value (Approximate):

Calories: 400-450, Fat: 30-35g, Protein: 20-25g, Carbs: 10-12g

Keto Breakfast Burrito

A keto breakfast burrito is a portable and tasty alternative that is excellent for those hectic mornings when you are on the road.

Prep Time: 10 minutes | Cooking Time: 5-7 minutes | Total Time: 15-17 minutes | Serving Size: 1

Ingredients:

- 1 low-carb tortilla
- 2-3 eggs, scrambled
- ¼ cup shredded cheese
- 2-3 slices cooked sausage, crumbled
- ¼ avocado, sliced
- 2 tablespoons salsa

Method of Preparation:

1. The low-carb tortilla can be warmed in a microwave or dry skillet.
2. In a separate skillet, scramble the eggs and cook until set.
3. Layer the scrambled eggs, cheese, sausage, avocado, and salsa onto the tortilla
4. Fold the tortilla tightly and enjoy!

Nutritional Value (Approximate):

Calories: 400-450, Fat: 30-35g, Protein: 25-30g, Carbs: 5-7g

Keto Egg Muffins

Keto egg muffins are a convenient and customizable breakfast option that can be prepared ahead of time and reheated throughout the week. They are fantastic grab-and-go lunch for busy mornings.

Prep Time: 10 minutes | Cooking Time: 20-25 minutes | Total Time: 30-35 minutes | Serving Size: 6 muffins

Ingredients:

- 6 big eggs
- ½ cup shredded cheese
- ½ cup chopped vegetables (spinach, mushrooms, bell peppers, onions) or cooked bacon crumbles
- Salt and pepper to taste

Method of Preparation:

1. Preheat oven to 350°F (175°C).
2. Use cooking spray or butter to grease a muffin pan.
3. Beat eggs, pepper, and salt together in a big basin.
4. Add cheese and your preferred ingredients and stir.
5. Evenly distribute the mixture among the muffin pans.
6. Bake the egg muffins for 20 to 25 minutes, or until they are set and have a golden brown hue.
7. Before taking from the muffin tin and serving, allow it cool somewhat.

Nutritional Value (Per Muffin):

Calories: 150-200, Fat: 12-15g, Protein: 10-12g, Carbs: 1-2g

Cloud Eggs

Cloud eggs are a light and fluffy breakfast choice that is both visually pleasing and delicious. The fluffy egg whites create a unique texture, while the creamy yolk adds richness and flavor.

Prep Time: 5 minutes | Cooking Time: 10-12 minutes | Total Time: 15-17 minutes | Serving Size: 2

Ingredients:

- 4 big eggs, separated
- Salt and pepper to taste

Method of Preparation:

1. Preheat oven to 400°F (200°C)
2. Line a baking sheet with parchment paper
3. In a large basin, whip the egg whites with an electric mixer until stiff peaks form
4. Season the egg whites with salt and pepper
5. Spoon the egg whites onto the prepared baking sheet, making two mounds with a well in the center of each
6. Carefully insert one egg yolk in the center of each egg white mound
7. Bake for 10-12 minutes or until the egg whites are golden and the yolks are set
8. Serve immediately

Nutritional Value (Per Serving):

Calories: 150-180, Fat: 10-12g, Protein: 12-14g, Carbs: 1-2g

Keto Granola

Keto granola is a delicious and crispy option for breakfast or snacking that is appropriate for anyone on a high-keto diet. Made with unsweetened coconut flakes, almonds, and seeds, it provides a good amount of fiber, protein, and fats.

Prep Time: 10 minutes | Cooking Time: 15-20 minutes | Total Time: 25-30 minutes | Serving Size: 4-6

Ingredients:

- 1 cup mixed nuts (almonds, walnuts, pecans)
- ½ cup seeds (pumpkin seeds, sunflower seeds, chia seeds)
- ½ cup unsweetened coconut flakes
- 2 teaspoons melted coconut oil
- 1 tablespoon sweetener of choice (e.g., stevia, monk fruit)
- 1 teaspoon cinnamon

Method of Preparation

1. Preheat oven to 300°F (150°C)
2. In a large dish combine nuts, seeds coconut flakes cinnamon, and sweetness
3. Drizzle with melted coconut oil and toss to coat evenly
4. Arrange the ingredients in a single layer on a parchment paper-lined baking sheet.

5. Bake for fifteen to twenty minutes, stirring frequently, until fragrant and golden brown.
6. Before storing in an airtight container, allow it cool fully.

Nutritional Value (Per Serving):

Calories: 200-250, Fat: 18-22g, Protein: 5-7g, Carbs: 5-7g

Keto Chaffles

Keto chaffles are a versatile and delicious breakfast choice that can be personalized with numerous toppings. Made with just two basic ingredients - eggs and cheese - they are a quick and easy way to enjoy a crispy and cheesy treat while staying in ketosis

---

Prep Time: 5 minutes | Cooking Time: 5-7 minutes | Total Time: 10-12 minutes | Serving Size: 2 chaffless

---

Ingredients:

- 1 big egg
- ½ cup shredded cheese (cheddar mozzarella or a mix)

Method of Preparation

1. Preheat a small waffle iron
2. In a small bowl mix together the egg and cheese
3. Transfer half of the mixture to the waffle iron that is heated.
4. Cook for three to four minutes, or until crispy and golden brown.
5. Repeat with the remaining batter
6. Serve immediately with your favorite keto-friendly toppings

Nutritional Value (Per Chaffle):

Calories: 200-250, Fat: 15-18g, Protein 12-15g, Carbs 1-2g

Chapter 5. Lunch

Bunless Burger Bowl

Are you trying to keep to your hyper ketosis diet but you have a craving for a juicy burger? This Bunless Burger Bowl offers all of the delight of a traditional American burger, but without the traditional bun that is loaded with carbohydrates. This lunch choice is not only fast and simple to cook, but it is also very flavorful and packed with protein.

Prep Time: 10 minutes | Cooking Time: 10-12 minutes | Total Time: 20-22 minutes | Serving Size: 1

Ingredients:

- 1/2-pound ground beef (80/20 blend or leaner)
- Salt and pepper to taste
- 1 tablespoon olive oil or avocado oil
- 2 cups mixed greens
- 1/4 avocado, sliced
- 2 slices cooked bacon, crumbled
- 1/4 cup shredded cheddar cheese
- Sugar-free ketchup or mustard, to taste

Method of Preparation:

1. Season the ground beef with salt and pepper. Shape into a patty.
2. In a skillet, heat the oil over medium-high heat. Cook the patties until they are cooked through, between five and seven minutes on each side.
3. In a bowl, combine the mixed greens, avocado, bacon, and cheese.
4. Top the salad with the cooked burger patty.
5. Drizzle with sugar-free ketchup or mustard, if preferred.

Nutritional Value (Approximate):

Calories: 500-600, Fat: 40-50g, Protein: 30-35g, Carbs: 5-7g

Buffalo Chicken Salad

This spicy and delicious salad is a wonderful keto-friendly lunch choice. The creamy buffalo sauce coupled with the soft shredded chicken delivers a taste explosion that will leave you wanting more.

Prep Time: 15 minutes | Cooking Time: 10-12 minutes | Total Time: 25-27 minutes | Serving Size: 2

Ingredients:

- 1 pound boneless, skinless chicken breasts
- Salt and pepper to taste
- 1/2 cup buffalo sauce (make sure it's sugar-free)
- 1/4 cup mayonnaise

- 1/4 cup crumbled blue cheese
- 1/4 cup chopped celery
- 2 tablespoons chopped green onions
- Lettuce leaves or mixed greens, for serving

Method of Preparation:

1. Add salt and pepper to the chicken breasts for seasoning.
2. Grill or poach the chicken until cooked through. Shred the chicken.
3. In a bowl, mix the shredded chicken, buffalo sauce, mayonnaise, blue cheese, celery, and green onions.
4. Wrapped in lettuce leaves or served over a bed of lettuce, this chicken salad tastes great.

Nutritional Value (Per Serving):

Calories: 350-400, Fat: 25-30g, Protein: 30-35g, Carbs: 5-7g

Salmon Salad Lettuce Wraps

These Salmon Salad Lettuce Wraps are a light and refreshing lunch choice that's filled with healthy fats and protein. The flaked salmon, mixed with fresh herbs and vegetables, produces a tasty and fulfilling lunch that is excellent for a warm day.

Prep Time: 15 minutes | Cooking Time: 0 minutes | Total Time: 15 minutes | Serving Size: 2

Ingredients:

- One can (14.75 ounces) of salmon, drained and flaked
- 1/4 cup mayonnaise
- 1/4 cup chopped celery
- 1/4 cup chopped red onion
- 2 tablespoons chopped fresh dill
- 1 tablespoon lemon juice
- Salt and pepper to taste
- 4 big lettuce leaves

Method of Preparation

1. In a medium bowl, mix the flakes of salmon, mayonnaise, celery, red onion, dill, lemon juice, salt, and pepper
2. Mix until completely blended
3. After spreading the salmon salad over the lettuce leaves, tightly wrap.

Nutritional Value (Per Serving):

Calories: 300-350, Fat: 25-30g, Protein: 15-20g, Carbs: 5-7g

Avocado Shrimp Ceviche

This tangy and delicious ceviche is a fantastic light lunch alternative, particularly during the warmer months. The mix of fresh shrimp, creamy avocado, and zesty lime juice delivers a blast of flavor that is both gratifying and keto-friendly.

Prep Time: 20 minutes | Cooking Time: 0 minutes (needs marinating time) | Total Time: 20 minutes prep + 30 minutes marinating | Serving Size: 2

Ingredients:

- 1-pound cooked shrimp, peeled and deveined
- 1 ripe avocado, chopped
- 1/2 cup chopped red onion
- 1/4 cup chopped fresh cilantro
- 1/4 cup lime juice
- 1 jalapeño jalapeno, seeded and coarsely chopped (optional)
- Salt and pepper to taste

Method of Preparation

1. In a medium bowl, mix the shrimp, avocado, red onion, cilantro, lime juice, jalapeño (if using), salt, and pepper.
2. Toss lightly to blend
3. Cover and chill for at least 30 minutes to enable the flavors to mingle
4. Serve chilly

Nutritional Value (Per Serving):

Calories: 300-350, Fat: 20-25g, Protein: 25-30g, Carbs: 5-7g

Keto Cobb Salad

A traditional Cobb salad gets a keto twist in this tasty and fulfilling lunch alternative. Packed with protein, healthy fats, and fresh veggies, it's a balanced meal that will leave you feeling full and invigorated.

Prep Time: 20 minutes | Cooking Time: 10-15 minutes (for grilling chicken or steak) | Total Time: 30-35 minutes | Serving Size: 1

Ingredients:

- 4 ounces grilled chicken or steak, sliced
- 2 slices cooked bacon, crumbled
- 2 hard-boiled eggs, sliced
- 1/2 avocado, diced
- 1/4 cup crumbled blue cheese
- 2 cups mixed greens
- Keto-friendly dressing of your choice

Method of Preparation:

1. Grill or grill the chicken or steak to your chosen degree of doneness. Slice and put aside
2. Arrange the mixed greens on a platter
3. Top with the sliced chicken or steak bacon hard-boiled eggs avocado blue cheese and your favorite keto-friendly dressing

Nutritional Value (Approximate):

Calories: 500-600, Fat: 40-50g, Protein: 30-35g, Carbs: 5-7g

Zucchini Noodles with Pesto and Chicken

Zucchini noodles, sometimes known as "zoodles," provide a light and refreshing substitute for traditional pasta, which makes this dish a great low-carb lunch with an Italian flair. The colorful handmade basil pesto offers a blast of flavor, while the grilled chicken delivers a fulfilling amount of protein.

Prep Time: 15 minutes | Cooking Time: 10-12 minutes | Total Time: 25-27 minutes | Serving Size: 2

Ingredients:

- 2 medium zucchini, spiralized into noodles
- One boneless, skinless chicken breast, grilled and sliced
- 1/4 cup fresh basil leaves
- 2 tablespoons pine nuts
- 2 cloves garlic, minced
- 1/4 cup olive oil
- 1/4 cup grated Parmesan cheese
- Salt and pepper to taste

Method of Preparation:

1. To create the pesto, put basil, pine nuts, garlic, olive oil, and Parmesan cheese in a food processor or blender. Pulse until smooth, adding additional olive oil if required to attain desired consistency. Season with salt and pepper.
2. Heat a skillet over medium heat. Add the zucchini noodles and simmer for 2-3 minutes, or until slightly softened but still al dente.
3. Toss the zucchini noodles with the pesto and grilled chicken.
4. Serve immediately, garnished with more Parmesan cheese if preferred.

Nutritional Value (Per Serving):

Calories: 400-450, Fat: 30-35g, Protein: 25-30g, Carbs: 10-12g

Cauliflower Rice Stir-Fry

Cauliflower rice is a flexible and low-carb replacement for regular rice, making it a mainstay in ketogenic diets. This stir-fry dish allows for infinite personalization with your favorite veggies and protein, making a delectable and healthy meal that's fast and simple to make.

Prep Time: 15 minutes | Cooking Time: 10-12 minutes | Total Time: 25-27 minutes | Serving Size: 2

Ingredients:

- 1 head cauliflower, riced
- 1 tablespoon olive oil or avocado oil
- 1/2 cup chopped onion
- 1 cup mixed veggies (bell peppers, broccoli florets, snap peas, etc.)
- 1/2 pound protein of choice (chicken, beef, shrimp, or tofu), cooked and sliced
- 1/4 cup low-sodium soy sauce (or coconut aminos for a soy-free alternative)
- 1 tablespoon oyster sauce (optional)
- 1 teaspoon sesame oil
- Salt and pepper to taste

Method of Preparation:

1. On medium-high heat, heat the oil in a big pan or wok.
2. Add the onion and heat until softened, approximately 3 minutes
3. Add the mixed veggies and protein and simmer until tender-crisp around 5 minutes
4. Add the cauliflower rice and simmer for 2-3 minutes or until cooked through
5. Combine the sesame oil and oyster sauce (if using) in a small bowl.
6. Drizzle the stir-fry with the sauce and mix to coat.
7. Serve right away after adding salt and pepper to taste.

Nutritional Value (Per Serving):

Calories: 300-400 (varies based on protein and veggies), Fat: 20-25g, Protein: 20-30g, Carbs: 10-15g

Keto Chili

This warm and cozy chili is a keto dieter's dream, filled with flavor and excellent for a full lunch or supper. The mix of ground beef, spices, and a hint of tomato paste makes a rich and flavorful meal that will warm you from the inside out.

Prep Time: 15 minutes | Cooking Time: 30-40 minutes | Total Time: 45-55 minutes | Serving Size: 4

Ingredients:

- 1 pound ground beef (80/20 blend or leaner)
- 1 onion, chopped
- 1 green bell pepper, chopped
- 2 cloves garlic, minced
- 1 tablespoon chili powder
- 1 teaspoon cumin

- 1/2 teaspoon paprika
- 1/4 teaspoon cayenne pepper (optional)
- 1 (14.5 ounces) can of chopped tomatoes, undrained
- 1 (15 ounce) can tomato sauce
- 1 tablespoon tomato paste
- 1 cup beef broth
- Salt and pepper to taste
- Shredded cheddar cheese with sour cream, for serving

Method of Preparation

1. Brown the ground beef in a large saucepan over medium heat. Drain off any excess grease
2. Add the onion and bell pepper and sauté until softened approximately 5 minutes
3. Add the garlic chili powder cumin paprika and cayenne pepper (if using) and sauté for 1 minute longer
4. Stir in the chopped tomatoes tomato sauce tomato paste and beef broth
5. Season with salt and pepper to taste
6. Bring to a boil then decrease heat and simmer for 30-40 minutes or until thickened
7. Serve warm, along with sour cream and shredded cheese.

Nutritional Value (Per Serving):

Calories: 350-400, Fat: 25-30g, Protein: 25-30g, Carbs: 8-10g

Tuna Salad Stuffed Avocado

This simple but fulfilling meal is a fantastic way to enjoy the creamy sweetness of avocado and the protein-packed tuna salad. It's a fast and simple supper that's great for individuals following a hyper ketosis diet.

Prep Time: 10 minutes | Cooking Time: 0 minutes | Total Time: 10 minutes | Serving Size: 1

Ingredients

- 1 ripe avocado, halved and pitted
- One (5 ounce) can of tuna in water, drained
- 2 tablespoons mayonnaise
- 1 tablespoon chopped celery
- 1 tablespoon chopped red onion
- 1 teaspoon Dijon mustard
- Salt and pepper to taste

Method of Preparation:

1. In a medium bowl, mix the tuna, mayonnaise, celery, red onion, Dijon mustard, salt, and pepper. Mix well
2. Fill each avocado half with the tuna salad mixture
3. Serve immediately

Nutritional Value (Approximate):

Calories: 400-450, Fat: 35-40g, Protein: 20-25g, Carbs: 5-7g

Keto Pizza Chaffles

Chaffles, a wonderful blend of cheese and eggs, give a crispy and cheesy foundation for a keto-friendly pizza experience. This dish lets you indulge in your pizza desires without losing your hyper ketosis aims.

Prep Time: 5 minutes | Cooking Time: 5-7 minutes per chaffle | Total Time: 10-12 minutes | Serving Size: 1 (makes 2 chaffles)

Ingredients:

- 1 big egg
- 1/2 cup shredded mozzarella cheese
- 2 tablespoons sugar-free pizza sauce
- 1/4 cup shredded mozzarella cheese, for topping
- Pizza toppings that are keto-friendly (pepperoni, mushrooms, olives, etc.)

Method of Preparation:

1. Preheat a small waffle iron
2. In a small bowl mix together the egg and 1/2 cup of mozzarella cheese
3. Transfer half of the mixture to the waffle iron that is heated.
4. Cook for three to four minutes, or until crispy and golden brown.
5. Repeat with the remaining batter
6. Top each chaffle with pizza sauce, extra mozzarella cheese, and your favorite toppings
7. Return the chaffles to the waffle iron and cook for one to two minutes, or until the cheese is bubbling and melted.

Nutritional Value (Per Serving):

Calories: 300-400 (varies based on toppings), Fat: 20-25g, Protein: 15-20g, Carbs: 3-5g

Chicken Fajita Salad

This vivid and tasty salad is a fiesta of textures and sensations, ideal for a light but fulfilling keto lunch. The grilled chicken strips give a lean protein source, while the colorful bell peppers and onions supply critical vitamins and antioxidants. The creamy avocado provides a hint of richness, and the tangy lime vinaigrette ties it all together.

Prep Time: 15 minutes | Cooking Time: 10-12 minutes | Total Time: 25-27 minutes | Serving Size: 2

Ingredients:

- 1-pound boneless, skinless chicken breasts, split into strips
- 1 tablespoon olive oil
- 1/2 teaspoon chili powder
- 1/2 teaspoon cumin
- 1/4 teaspoon garlic powder
- 1/4 teaspoon salt
- 1/4 teaspoon black pepper
- 1 bell pepper (any color), sliced
- 1/2 onion, sliced
- 4 cups mixed greens
- 1 avocado, sliced
- Lime Vinaigrette:

- 1/4 cup olive oil
- 2 tablespoons lime juice
- 1 tablespoon chopped fresh cilantro
- 1 clove garlic, minced
- Salt and pepper to taste

Method of Preparation:

1. In a bowl, mix chicken strips with olive oil, chili powder, cumin, garlic powder, salt, and pepper. Toss to coat.
2. Heat a grill or skillet over medium-high heat. Grill the chicken strips for 5-7 minutes on each side, or until cooked through.
3. Prepare the lime vinaigrette by combining all the ingredients in a small dish while the chicken is cooking.
4. In a large bowl, combine the mixed greens, bell pepper, onion, and avocado.
5. Top with the grilled chicken and sprinkle with the lime vinaigrette.
6. Toss to coat and serve immediately.

Nutritional Value (Per Serving):

Calories: 400-450, Fat: 30-35g, Protein: 30-35g, Carbs: 10-12g

Egg Salad Lettuce Wraps

This traditional egg salad recipe is a quick and easy lunch option that works well for anyone on a high-keto diet. Crisp lettuce leaves are filled with a tasty and high-protein dish of creamy egg salad that has been prepared with mayonnaise, mustard, and seasonings.

Prep Time: 10 minutes | Cooking Time: 10-12 minutes (for hard-boiling eggs) | Total Time: 20-22 minutes | Serving Size: 2

Ingredients:

- 6 big eggs
- 1/4 cup mayonnaise
- 1 tablespoon Dijon mustard
- 1 tablespoon chopped fresh chives
- 1/4 teaspoon salt
- 1/4 teaspoon black pepper
- 4 big lettuce leaves

Method of Preparation:

1. In a saucepan, arrange the eggs in a single layer. Pour in enough cold water to come up to about an inch over the eggs.
2. Put the water over medium-high heat and bring it to a rolling boil.
3. Once boiling, remove from the heat, place a lid on the pot, and let the eggs settle for ten to twelve minutes.
4. Drain the boiling water and immediately pour cold water over the eggs to chill them down.
5. Peel the eggs and slice them into little pieces.
6. Add the diced eggs, mustard, mayonnaise, chives, salt, and pepper to a bowl. Mix well.
7. Spoon the egg salad onto the lettuce leaves and wrap securely.
8. Serve immediately.

Nutritional Value (Per Serving):

Calories: 350-400, Fat: 30-35g, Protein: 15-20g, Carbs: 3-5g

Steak Salad with Blue Cheese Dressing

This rich and savory salad is a wonderful keto-friendly lunch option for steak fans. The combination of grilled steak, crumbled blue cheese, and juicy cherry tomatoes produces a tasty and nutritious lunch that is high in protein and healthy fats.

Prep Time: 10 minutes | Cooking Time: 10-12 minutes (for grilling steak) | Total Time: 20-22 minutes | Serving Size: 1

Ingredients:

- 4 ounces steak (sirloin, flank, or your preferred cut)
- Salt and pepper to taste
- 1 tablespoon olive oil or avocado oil
- 2 cups mixed greens
- 1/4 cup crumbled blue cheese
- 1/2 cup cherry tomatoes, halved
- Blue Cheese Dressing:
- 1/4 cup mayonnaise
- 1/4 cup sour cream
- 1/4 cup crumbled blue cheese
- 1 tablespoon lemon juice
- 1/4 teaspoon garlic powder
- Salt and pepper to taste

Method of Preparation

1. Season the meat with salt and pepper
2. Heat the oil in a pan or grill over medium-high heat Cook the steak to your desired degree of doneness
3. While the steak is cooking create the blue cheese dressing by mixing together all the ingredients in a small dish
4. In a large dish combine the mixed greens cherry tomatoes and crumbled blue cheese
5. Top with the cut steak and sprinkle with the blue cheese dressing
6. Toss to coat and serve immediately

Nutritional Value (Approximate):

Calories: 500-600, Fat: 40-45g, Protein: 30-35g, Carbs: 5-7g

Keto BLT Wraps

The traditional BLT sandwich gets a keto-friendly update in these tasty wraps. Crispy bacon, fresh lettuce, and juicy tomatoes are packed in a low-carb tortilla or lettuce leaves for a filling and convenient lunch choice.

Prep Time: 10 minutes | Cooking Time: 5-7 minutes (for cooking bacon) | Total Time: 15-17 minutes | Serving Size: 2

Ingredients:

- 4 slices bacon

- 4 large lettuce leaves or 2 low-carb tortillas
- 1 big tomato, cut
- Mayonnaise, to taste

Method of Preparation

1. Cook the bacon in a pan over medium heat until crispy Drain on a paper towel-lined platter
2. If using tortillas toast them slightly in a dry skillet or microwave
3. Drizzle the tortillas or lettuce leaves with mayonnaise.
4. Layer the bacon lettuce and tomato slices
5. Roll up tightly and enjoy

Nutritional Value (Per Serving):

Calories: 300-350, Fat: 25-30g, Protein: 10-12g, Carbs: 3-5g

Broccoli and Cheese Soup

This comforting, creamy soup is surprisingly keto-friendly and perfect for a chilly day. The mix of broccoli, cheese, and heavy cream provides a rich and pleasant taste that will warm you from the inside out.

Prep Time: 10 minutes | Cooking Time: 20-25 minutes | Total Time: 30-35 minutes | Serving Size: 4

Ingredients:

- 1 head of broccoli, chopped
- 1/2 onion, chopped
- 2 cloves garlic, minced
- 4 cups chicken broth or veggie broth
- 1 cup heavy cream
- 1 cup shredded cheddar cheese
- Salt and pepper to taste

Method of Preparation:

1. Melt the butter in a big skillet over medium heat. Add the onion and cook for about five minutes, or until softened.
2. Add the garlic and simmer for 1 minute longer
3. Add the broccoli chicken broth/vegetable broth salt and pepper Bring to a boil then decrease heat and simmer for 15-20 minutes or until the broccoli is tender
4. Using an immersion blender or a conventional blender purée the soup until smooth
5. Add the cheese and heavy cream and stir. Cook until the soup is well heated and the cheese is melted over medium heat.
6. Serve hot

Nutritional Value (Per Serving):

Calories: 300-350, Fat: 25-30g, Protein: 10-12g, Carbs: 5-7g

Chapter 6. Dinner

Garlic Butter Shrimp Scampi with Zoodles

This meal reimagines the classic Shrimp Scampi, swapping carb-heavy pasta with zucchini noodles (zoodles) for a lighter, keto-friendly variation. The delicious shrimp, soaked in a fragrant garlic butter sauce, create a symphony of tastes that will take you to the heart of Italy, all while keeping you securely in ketosis.

Prep Time: 15 minutes | Cooking Time: 10 minutes | Total Time: 25 minutes | Serving Size: 2

Ingredients:

- 1-pound big shrimp, peeled and deveined
- 4 tablespoons butter
- 4 cloves garlic, minced
- 1/4 cup dry white wine (optional)
- 1/4 cup chicken broth
- 2 teaspoons lemon juice
- 2 teaspoons chopped fresh parsley
- Salt and pepper to taste
- 2 medium zucchini, spiralized into noodles

Method of Preparation:

1. Heat a large pan over medium heat and melt two tablespoons of butter. When the shrimp are pink and fully cooked, add them and heat them for two to three minutes on each side. Take out and set aside the shrimp from the skillet.
2. Heat the last two tablespoons of butter in the same pan. Add the garlic and cook for about 30 seconds, or until fragrant. Take care not to scorch the garlic.
3. Pour the chicken stock and white wine (if using) into the skillet. After bringing to a simmer, cook for two to three minutes, or until half of the liquid has evaporated.
4. Add the parsley and lemon juice and stir. To taste, add salt and pepper for seasoning.
5. Put the shrimp back in the pan and toss them around to cover with sauce.
6. Meanwhile, prepare a separate skillet over medium heat. Add the zucchini noodles and simmer for 2-3 minutes, or until slightly softened but still al dente.
7. Spoon the shrimp and sauce on top of the zucchini noodles.

Nutritional Value (Per Serving):

Calories: 400-450, Fat: 30-35g, Protein: 30-35g, Carbs: 5-7g

Cheeseburger Salad

This deconstructed cheeseburger salad is a fun and savory way to enjoy all the usual burger toppings without the carb-heavy bun. It's a wonderful keto-friendly lunch or supper option that's filled with protein and healthy fats.

Prep Time: 15 minutes | Cooking Time: 10-12 minutes | Total Time: 25-27 minutes | Serving Size: 1

Ingredients:

- 1/2 pound ground beef (80/20 blend or leaner)
- Salt and pepper to taste
- 1 tablespoon olive oil or avocado oil
- 2 cups mixed greens
- 1/4 cup shredded cheddar cheese
- 2-3 dill pickle slices, chopped
- 1/4 red onion, thinly sliced
- 2-3 slices tomato
- Sugar-Free "Special Sauce":
- 1/4 cup mayonnaise
- 1 tablespoon sugar-free ketchup
- 1 teaspoon yellow mustard
- 1/2 teaspoon dill pickle relish

Method of Preparation

1. Season the ground beef with salt and pepper. Shape into a patty
2. Heat the oil in a pan over medium-high heat Cook the patties for approximately 5-7 minutes on each side or until cooked through
3. While the patty is cooking, create the special sauce by mixing all the ingredients in a small dish
4. In a large bowl, combine the mixed greens, cheese, pickles, onion, and tomato
5. Place the cooked burger patty on top of the salad.
6. Drizzle with the special sauce

Nutritional Value (Approximate):

Calories: 500-600, Fat: 40-45g, Protein: 30-35g, Carbs: 5-7g

Baked Salmon with Creamy Spinach

This simple but gorgeous meal is a fantastic keto-friendly supper choice that is both nutritional and tasty. The baked salmon is flaky and tasty, while the creamy spinach side dish adds a hint of richness and pleasure

Prep Time: 10 minutes | Cooking Time: 15-20 minutes | Total Time: 25-30 minutes | Serving Size: 2

Ingredients:

- 2 salmon fillets (6-8 ounces each)
- 1 tablespoon olive oil
- 1/2 teaspoon salt
- 1/4 teaspoon black pepper
- 1/2 lemon, sliced
- 10 ounces fresh spinach
- 2 tablespoons butter
- 2 cloves garlic, minced
- 1/4 cup heavy cream
- 1/4 cup grated Parmesan cheese
- Salt and pepper to taste

Method of Preparation:

1. Preheat oven to 400°F (200°C)
2. Arrange the salmon fillets onto a parchment paper-lined baking sheet.
3. Season the salmon with salt and pepper and drizzle with olive oil.
4. Top each fillet with a couple of lemon wedges
5. Bake the salmon for fifteen to twenty minutes, or until it is cooked through and flake readily with a fork.
6. While the salmon is baking, melt the butter in a large pan over medium heat
7. Add the garlic and heat until fragrant for 30 seconds
8. Add the spinach and simmer until wilted around 2-3 minutes
9. Stir in the heavy cream and Parmesan cheese Cook for 1-2 minutes longer, or until the sauce thickens
10. Season with salt and pepper to taste
11. Serve the cooked salmon with the creamy spinach

Nutritional Value (Per Serving):

Calories: 500-550, Fat: 40-45g, Protein: 30-35g, Carbs: 5-7g

Chicken Fajitas

These sizzling chicken fajitas bring the vivid taste of Mexico to your keto table. The soft chicken pieces, bright bell peppers, and onions produce a delightful and gratifying supper that is excellent for sharing with family and friends

Prep Time: 15 minutes | Cooking Time: 10-12 minutes | Total Time: 25-27 minutes | Serving Size: 4

Ingredients

- 1-pound boneless skinless chicken breasts cut into thin strips

- 1 tablespoon olive oil
- 1/2 teaspoon chili powder
- 1/2 teaspoon cumin
- 1/4 teaspoon garlic powder
- 1/4 teaspoon salt
- 1/4 teaspoon black pepper
- 1 bell pepper (any color) cut
- 1 onion sliced
- 8 big lettuce leaves
- Guacamole sour cream and salsa for serving

Method of Preparation

1. In a dish mix chicken strips with olive oil chili powder cumin garlic powder salt and pepper Toss to coat
2. Heat a large skillet or grill pan over medium-high heat Add the chicken and cook for 5-7 minutes or until cooked through
3. Add the bell pepper and onion to the pan and simmer for 3-4 minutes or until softened
4. Serve the chicken and veggies in lettuce wraps with guacamole sour cream and salsa

Nutritional Value (Per Serving):

Calories: 350-400, Fat: 25-30g, Protein: 30-35g, Carbs: 5-7g

Cauliflower Mac and Cheese

A tasty keto alternative to regular mac & cheese, this dish utilizes cauliflower as a low-carb replacement for pasta.

Prep Time: 15 minutes | Cook Time: 25 minutes | Total Time: 40 minutes | Serving Size: 4 servings

Ingredients:

- One big head of cauliflower, chopped into florets
- 1 cup heavy cream
- 2 cups shredded cheddar cheese
- ½ cup grated Parmesan cheese
- 2 ounces cream cheese
- 1 tsp garlic powder
- Salt and pepper to taste
- 2 tbsp butter

Method of Preparation:

1. Preheat your oven to 375°F (190°C).
2. Steam the cauliflower florets until soft, approximately 5-7 minutes.
3. Melt the butter in a saucepan and mix in the cream cheese and heavy cream. Incorporate the cream and melt the cream cheese by stirring.
4. Add the shredded cheddar, Parmesan, and garlic powder. Stir until the cheese is totally melted and creamy.
5. Toss the cooked cauliflower in the cheese sauce.
6. Transfer the cauliflower mixture to a baking dish and bake for 20 minutes until bubbling and brown on top.

Nutritional Value (Per Serving):

Calories: 340, Fat: 30g, Carbohydrates: 7g, Protein: 14g

Bacon-Wrapped Asparagus

A beautiful combination of crispy bacon and soft asparagus, this meal gives a rush of flavor with every mouthful. It's a simple but exquisite keto snack or side dish that's low in carbohydrates and high in fats.

Prep Time: 10 minutes | Cook Time: 20 minutes | Total Time: 30 minutes | Serving Size: 4 servings

Ingredients:

- 16 asparagus spears
- 8 strips of bacon
- 1 tsp olive oil
- Salt and pepper to taste

Method of Preparation:

1. Preheat your oven to 400°F (200°C).
2. Trim the ends of the asparagus stalks and mix them with olive oil, salt, and pepper.
3. Wrap each bundle of two asparagus stalks with a piece of bacon.
4. Place the wrapped asparagus on a baking sheet and bake for 18-20 minutes, or until the bacon is crispy.

Nutritional Value (Per Serving):

Calories: 250, Fat: 20g, Carbohydrates: 2g, Protein: 12g

Sheet Pan Chicken and Veggies

This one-pan recipe is excellent for a hassle-free, nutritious keto evening. Chicken and bright veggies like broccoli, Brussels sprouts, and bell peppers are roasted together and seasoned to perfection, making it both healthful and delectable.

Prep Time: 10 minutes | Cook Time: 25-30 minutes | Total Time: 40 minutes | Serving Size: 4 servings

Ingredients:

- 4 chicken thighs or breasts
- 1 cup broccoli florets
- 1 cup Brussels sprouts, halved
- 1 red bell pepper, sliced
- 1 tsp garlic powder
- 1 tsp paprika
- 2 tbsp olive oil
- Salt and pepper to taste

Method of Preparation:

1. Preheat your oven to 400°F (200°C).
2. Toss the veggies with olive oil, garlic powder, paprika, salt, and pepper.
3. Arrange the vegetables and chicken on a sheet pan.
4. Roast for 25-30 minutes until the chicken achieves an internal temperature of 165°F (75°C) and the veggies are soft.

Nutritional Value (Per Serving):

Calories: 380, Fat: 24g, Carbohydrates: 7g, Protein: 30g

Keto Meatballs with Marinara Sauce

These delicate meatballs are filled with flavor and served in a flavorful, sugar-free marinara sauce. Made with either beef or pork, this keto-friendly rendition of an Italian classic is excellent for supper or meal prep.

Prep Time: 15 minutes | Cook Time: 25 minutes | Total Time: 40 minutes | Serving Size: 4 servings

Ingredients:

- 1 pound ground beef or pork
- 1 egg
- ¼ cup grated Parmesan cheese
- 2 cloves garlic, minced
- 1 tsp Italian seasoning
- 1 ½ cups sugar-free marinara sauce
- 2 tbsp olive oil
- Salt and pepper to taste

Method of Preparation:

1. Preheat your oven to 375°F (190°C).
2. In a bowl, combine the ground beef, egg, Parmesan, garlic, Italian seasoning, salt, and pepper.
3. Form the mixture into meatballs.
4. Heat olive oil in a pan and cook the meatballs on both sides.
5. Transfer the browned meatballs to a baking sheet, top with marinara sauce, and bake for 20 minutes.

Nutritional Value (Per Serving):

Calories: 350, Fat: 26g, Carbohydrates: 6g, Protein: 20g

Steak with Roasted Garlic Cauliflower Mash

A delicious steak topped with creamy roasted garlic cauliflower mash is a full, savory, and keto-friendly supper choice. The cauliflower mash is a fantastic low-carb replacement for regular mashed potatoes.

Prep Time: 15 minutes | Cook Time: 25 minutes | Total Time: 40 minutes | Serving Size: 4 servings

Ingredients:

- 4 steaks (sirloin or ribeye)
- 1 huge head of cauliflower
- 4 cloves garlic
- ½ cup thick cream
- 3 tbsp butter
- 2 tbsp olive oil
- Salt and pepper to taste

Method of Preparation:

1. Preheat your oven to 400°F (200°C).
2. Using olive oil, roast the garlic cloves for fifteen to twenty minutes, or until they become soft.
3. Steam the cauliflower florets until soft, approximately 10 minutes.
4. Add the roasted garlic, butter, and heavy cream to the cauliflower and blend until smooth.

5. Season the steaks with salt and pepper, then cook in a heated pan to your chosen doneness.
6. Serve the steak with cauliflower mash.

Nutritional Value (Per Serving):

Calories: 500, Fat: 35g, Carbohydrates: 8g, Protein: 38g

One-Pan Baked Chicken Parmesan

This keto-friendly variation on the traditional Chicken Parmesan utilizes almond flour and Parmesan cheese to coat the chicken, making it low-carb yet wonderfully tasty. Baked with marinara sauce and mozzarella, it's a simple, tasty weekday supper.

Prep Time: 10 minutes | Cook Time: 25 minutes | Total Time: 35 minutes | Serving Size: 4 servings

Ingredients:

- 4 boneless, skinless chicken breasts
- ½ cup almond flour
- ½ cup grated Parmesan cheese
- 1 tsp Italian seasoning
- 1 cup sugar-free marinara sauce
- 1 cup shredded mozzarella cheese
- 1 egg, beaten
- 2 tbsp olive oil
- Salt and pepper to taste

Method of Preparation:

1. Preheat your oven to 400°F (200°C).
2. Mix the almond flour, Parmesan, and Italian seasoning in a bowl.
3. Dip each chicken breast in the beaten egg, then coat with the almond flour mixture.
4. Heat olive oil in a pan and brown the chicken breasts on both sides, approximately 2-3 minutes on each side.
5. Transfer the chicken breasts to a baking sheet, pour marinara sauce over them, and sprinkle with mozzarella cheese.
6. Bake for twenty to twenty-five minutes, or until the cheese is melted and bubbling and the chicken is well cooked.

Nutritional Value (Per Serving):

Calories: 450, Fat: 30g, Carbohydrates: 7g, Protein: 35g

Philly Cheesesteak Stuffed Peppers

With the exception of the bread, these Philly Cheesesteak Stuffed Peppers are packed with all the flavors of the well-known sandwich. Bell peppers serve as a low-carb conduit for thinly sliced steak, sautéed onions, mushrooms, and melted cheese, making it a keto-friendly supper choice.

Prep Time: 15 minutes | Cook Time: 25 minutes | Total Time: 40 minutes | Serving Size: 4 serving

Ingredients:

- 4 big bell peppers, halves, and seeds removed
- One pounds thinly cut steak (ribeye or sirloin)
- 1 cup mushrooms, sliced
- 1 onion, thinly sliced
- 1 cup shredded provolone or mozzarella cheese
- 2 tbsp olive oil
- 1 tsp garlic powder
- Salt and pepper to taste

Method of Preparation:

1. Preheat your oven to 375°F (190°C).
2. In a pan, heat olive oil and sauté the onions, mushrooms, and garlic powder until soft.
3. Add the cut steak to the pan and heat until browned.
4. Place the bell pepper halves in a baking tray and fill each with the meat and veggie mixture.
5. Add some shredded cheese on top, then bake for fifteen to twenty minutes, or until the cheese melts and the peppers become tender.

Nutritional Value (Per Serving):

Calories: 380, Fat: 28g, Carbohydrates: 6g, Protein: 25g

Keto Egg Roll in a Bowl

This deconstructed egg roll gives all the taste of a classic egg roll without the carbohydrates. Ground pork, cabbage, and carrots are stir-fried with ginger, garlic, and soy sauce, making this a fast and simple keto supper.

Prep Time: 10 minutes | Cook Time: 15 minutes | Total Time: 25 minutes | Serving Size: 4 servings

Ingredients:

- 1 pound ground pork (or chicken)
- 1 small head of cabbage, shredded
- 1 cup shredded carrots
- 2 cloves garlic, minced
- 1 tbsp grated ginger
- 2 tbsp soy sauce or coconut aminos
- 2 tbsp sesame oil
- 1 tbsp olive oil
- Salt and pepper to taste
- Optional garnish: sesame seeds, sliced green onions

Method of Preparation:

1. In a big pan over medium heat, warm the olive oil.
2. Add the ground pork and sauté until browned, breaking it up as it cooks.
3. Stir in the garlic, ginger, cabbage, and carrots. Sauté until the veggies are soft.
4. Mix well after adding the sesame oil and soy sauce. Cook for a further 2-3 minutes.
5. Serve hot, topped with sesame seeds and green onions if preferred.

Nutritional Value (Per Serving):

Calories: 310, Fat: 23g, Carbohydrates: 8g, Protein: 18g

Grilled Salmon with Avocado Salsa

This fresh and healthful meal offers freshly grilled salmon topped with a zesty avocado salsa prepared with tomatoes, red onions, cilantro, and lime juice. It's a nutrient-packed, low-carb dinner that's high in heart-healthy fats.

Prep Time: 10 minutes | Cook Time: 15 minutes | Total Time: 25 minutes | Serving Size: 4 servings

Ingredients:

- 4 salmon fillets
- 1 tbsp olive oil
- 2 avocados, diced
- 1 tomato, diced
- ¼ red onion, coarsely chopped
- 2 tbsp fresh cilantro, chopped
- Juice of 1 lime
- Salt and pepper to taste

Method of Preparation:

1. Preheat your grill to medium-high heat.
2. Coat the salmon fillets in olive oil and sprinkle with salt and pepper.
3. Cook the salmon on the grill for 4-6 minutes per side, or until it is fully cooked.
4. In a bowl, add the chopped avocados, tomato, red onion, cilantro, lime juice, salt, and pepper to create the salsa.
5. Serve the grilled salmon topped with avocado salsa.

Nutritional Value (Per Serving):

Calories: 400, Fat: 28g, Carbohydrates: 6g, Protein: 30g

Buffalo Chicken Casserole

This hearty Buffalo Chicken Casserole combines shredded chicken, buffalo sauce, ranch dressing, and cheese for a filling and delicious keto-friendly meal. It's perfect for large gatherings like game days or family dinners.

Prep Time: 15 minutes | Cook Time: 30 minutes | Total Time: 45 minutes | Serving Size: 6 servings

---

Ingredients:

- 3 cups cooked, shredded chicken
- ½ cup buffalo sauce
- ½ cup ranch dressing (sugar-free)
- 1 cup shredded cheddar cheese
- 1 cup shredded mozzarella cheese
- 2 tbsp cream cheese
- 2 tbsp butter
- Salt and pepper to taste
- Optional garnish: chopped green onions or parsley

Method of Preparation:

1. Preheat your oven to 375°F (190°C).
2. The butter and cream cheese should be melted in a pan. Once combined, stir in the ranch dressing and buffalo sauce.
3. In a large bowl, combine the shredded chicken with the sauce mixture.
4. Transfer the mixture to a baking dish and sprinkle with the shredded cheese.
5. Bake for 25-30 minutes until bubbling and golden on top.
6. If desired, add parsley or green onions as a garnish.

Nutritional Value (Per Serving):

Calories: 420, Fat: 30g, Carbohydrates: 3g, Protein: 30g

Chapter 7. Poultry

Keto Lemon Garlic Butter Chicken Thighs

Juicy chicken thighs cooked in a zesty lemon garlic butter sauce are excellent for a fast and simple weekend supper. The rich aromas of garlic and butter mix with the freshness of lemon, producing a wonderful, keto-friendly recipe that the entire family will appreciate.

Prep Time: 10 minutes | Cook Time: 30 minutes | Total Time: 40 minutes | Serving Size: 4 servings

Ingredients:

- 4 bone-in, skin-on chicken thighs
- 4 tbsp unsalted butter
- 4 cloves garlic, minced
- 1 lemon, juiced
- 1 tsp lemon zest
- 1 tsp fresh thyme leaves
- Salt and pepper to taste

Method of Preparation:

1. Preheat your oven to 400°F (200°C).
2. Add salt and pepper to the chicken thighs for seasoning.
3. Melt two tablespoons of butter in a pan over medium heat. Place the chicken thighs skin side down and fry until golden brown, about 5 minutes.
4. Turn the thighs over and sprinkle with thyme, lemon zest, juice, and garlic.
5. After placing the pan in the oven, roast it for 25 to 30 minutes, or until the internal temperature of the chicken reaches 165°F.
6. Melt the remaining butter over the chicken thighs before serving.

Nutritional Value (per serving):

Calories: 380, Fat: 30g, Protein: 24g, Carbohydrates: 2g, Fiber: 0g, Net Carbs: 2g

Buffalo Chicken Wings

These crispy baked chicken wings are covered in a buttery buffalo sauce and served with keto-friendly ranch dressing and celery sticks. A keto staple, this dish gives the taste of regular wings without the carbohydrates.

Prep Time: 10 minutes | Cook Time: 45 minutes | Total Time: 55 minutes | Serving Size: 4 servings

Ingredients:

- 2 pounds of chicken wings
- 1 tsp baking powder
- ½ tsp garlic powder
- ½ tsp paprika
- Salt and pepper to taste
- ¼ cup unsalted butter
- ¼ cup buffalo sauce

- Keto ranch dressing and celery sticks for serving

Method of Preparation:

1. Preheat the oven to 400°F (200°C). Line a baking sheet with parchment paper to prepare it.
2. In a bowl, mix the wings with baking powder, garlic powder, paprika, salt, and pepper.
3. Spread the wings in a single layer on the baking sheet. Bake for 45 minutes, turning halfway through, until crispy.
4. In a skillet, heat butter and whisk in buffalo sauce.
5. Toss the cooked wings in the buffalo sauce and serve with keto ranch dressing and celery sticks.

Nutritional Value (per serving):

Calories: 390, Fat: 31g, Protein: 28g, Carbohydrates: 1g, Fiber: 0g, Net Carbs: 1g

Creamy Spinach-Stuffed Chicken Breast

This keto-friendly recipe has chicken breasts packed with a creamy combination of spinach, cream cheese, and parmesan, then baked till golden and soft. It's a cozy but sophisticated supper suited for any night of the week.

Prep Time: 15 minutes | Cook Time: 30 minutes | Total Time: 45 minutes | Serving Size: 4 servings

Ingredients:

- 4 boneless, skinless chicken breasts
- 4 ounces cream cheese, softened
- 1 cup fresh spinach, chopped
- ½ cup grated parmesan cheese
- 1 tsp garlic powder
- 1 tsp onion powder
- 1 tbsp olive oil
- Salt and pepper to taste

Method of Preparation:

1. Preheat the oven to 375°F (190°C).
2. In a bowl, combine cream cheese, spinach, parmesan, garlic powder, onion powder, salt, and pepper.
3. Slice each chicken breast lengthwise to make a pocket. Fill each breast with the mixture of spinach.
4. In a skillet that is oven safe, warm the olive oil over medium heat. The chicken breasts should be seared for 3–4 minutes on each side to brown them.
5. After the pan is placed in the oven, roast the chicken for twenty-five to thirty minutes, or until its internal temperature reaches 165°F.

Nutritional Value (per serving):

Calories: 320, Fat: 20g, Protein: 32g, Carbohydrates: 3g, Fiber: 1g, Net Carbs: 2g

Chicken Alfredo Zucchini Noodles

This meal has grilled chicken served over spiralized zucchini noodles, topped with a thick and creamy keto-friendly Alfredo sauce. It's a terrific low-carb alternative to regular spaghetti.

Prep Time: 15 minutes | Cook Time: 20 minutes | Total Time: 35 minutes | Serving Size: 4 servings

Ingredients:

- 4 boneless, skinless chicken breasts
- 4 medium zucchini, spiralized
- 1 cup heavy cream
- ½ cup grated parmesan cheese
- 2 tbsp unsalted butter
- 2 cloves garlic, minced
- Salt and pepper to taste
- 1 tbsp olive oil

Method of Preparation:

1. In a pan set over medium heat, warm the olive oil. After adding salt and pepper to the chicken, grill it for six to seven minutes on each side, or until it is cooked through. Put aside.
2. In another pan, heat butter and sauté garlic for 1-2 minutes. Add heavy cream and parmesan, stirring until the sauce thickens.
3. Add zucchini noodles to the sauce and stir for 2-3 minutes until coated.
4. Slice the grilled chicken and serve on top of the zucchini noodles.

Nutritional Value (per serving):

Calories: 380, Fat: 28g, Protein: 34g, Carbohydrates: 5g, Fiber: 2g, Net Carbs: 3g

Baked Pesto Chicken with Mozzarella

Chicken breasts covered with fresh basil pesto and mozzarella cheese, cooked until the cheese is bubbling and golden. This meal is packed with robust flavors, making it a perfect keto dinner choice.

Prep Time: 10 minutes | Cook Time: 25 minutes | Total Time: 35 minutes | Serving Size: 4 servings

Ingredients:

- 4 boneless, skinless chicken breasts
- ½ cup fresh basil pesto
- 1 cup shredded mozzarella cheese
- 1 tbsp olive oil
- Salt and pepper to taste

Method of Preparation:

1. Preheat the oven to 400°F (200°C).
2. Rub some salt and pepper on the chicken breasts.
3. Lightly warm up some olive oil in a pan.
4. Sear the chicken breasts for 3-4 minutes each side until browned.
5. Transfer to a baking dish, pour 2 tbsp of pesto on each breast, and top with shredded mozzarella.

6. Bake for 20-25 minutes until the chicken reaches an internal temperature of 165°F and the cheese is bubbling.

Nutritional Value (per serving):

Calories: 420, Fat: 30g, Protein: 32g, Carbohydrates: 2g, Fiber: 0g, Net Carbs: 2g

Keto Chicken Cordon Bleu

Chicken Cordon Bleu is a traditional recipe turned keto-friendly by using almond flour as a breading. This dish combines chicken breast folded with ham and Swiss cheese, cooked to crispy perfection, and overflowing with flavorful aromas.

Prep Time: 15 minutes | Cook Time: 30 minutes | Total Time: 45 minutes | Serving Size: 4 servings

---

Ingredients:

- 4 boneless, skinless chicken breasts
- 4 slices of ham
- 4 pieces of Swiss cheese
- 1 cup almond flour
- 2 big eggs
- 2 tbsp olive oil
- Salt and pepper to taste
- 1 tsp garlic powder
- 1 tsp paprika

Method of Preparation:

1. Preheat the oven to 375°F (190°C).
2. Place each chicken breast between two pieces of plastic wrap and pound to a uniform thickness.
3. Place a slice of Swiss cheese and ham on each chicken breast. Securely roll the chicken and use toothpicks to bind it.
4. Set up a breading station with one basin for beaten eggs and another for almond flour combined with garlic powder, paprika, salt, and pepper.
5. Coat each chicken roll first in the egg, then in the almond flour.
6. Put olive oil in a pan and heat it on medium-high. Sear each chicken roll for 2-3 minutes each side until golden brown.
7. Transfer to a baking sheet and bake for 25-30 minutes, or until the chicken reaches an internal temperature of 165°F.

Nutritional Value (per serving):

Calories: 350, Fat: 25g, Protein: 30g, Carbohydrates: 6g, Fiber: 2g, Net Carbs: 4g

Jalapeño Popper Chicken Casserole

This soothing dish blends shredded chicken with creamy cream cheese, fiery jalapeños, and melted cheddar cheese. It's a tasty, comforting dinner suited for keto dieters.

Prep Time: 10 minutes | Cook Time: 30 minutes | Total Time: 40 minutes | Serving Size: 6 servings

Ingredients:

- 2 cups shredded cooked chicken
- 8 oz cream cheese, softened
- 1 cup shredded cheddar cheese
- 1/4 cup chopped jalapeños (fresh or pickled)
- 1/2 cup sour cream
- 1/2 tsp garlic powder
- Salt and pepper to taste

Method of Preparation:

1. Preheat the oven to 375°F (190°C).
2. In a big bowl, combine shredded chicken, cream cheese, cheddar cheese, chopped jalapeños, sour cream, garlic powder, salt, and pepper, ensuring everything is well mixed.
3. Then, move the mixture into a baking dish that has been greased.
4. Bake for 25-30 minutes, or until the top is bubbling and golden brown.
5. Let cool slightly before serving.

Nutritional Value (per serving):

Calories: 320, Fat: 24g, Protein: 20g, Carbohydrates: 5g, Fiber: 1g, Net Carbs: 4g

Lemon Herb Roasted Chicken

This roasted chicken is seasoned with tangy lemon, garlic, and fresh herbs, and then baked to golden perfection. Served with keto-friendly roasted veggies, it's a wonderful and healthful supper choice.

Prep Time: 15 minutes | Cook Time: 1 hour 15 minutes | Total Time: 1 hour 30 minutes | Serving Size: 4 servings

Ingredients:

- 1 entire chicken (approximately 4-5 lbs)
- 2 tbsp olive oil
- 1 lemon, quartered
- 4 cloves garlic, minced
- 2 tbsp fresh rosemary, chopped
- 2 tbsp fresh thyme, chopped
- Salt and pepper to taste

Method of Preparation:

1. Preheat the oven to 400°F (200°C).
2. Pat the chicken dry with paper towels. Coat the chicken completely with olive oil.
3. Season the interior of the chicken with salt and pepper. Stuff the cavity with lemon quarters, garlic, rosemary, and thyme.

4. Rub the exterior of the chicken with salt, pepper, and extra rosemary and thyme.
5. Arrange the chicken in a roasting pan on a rack. Roast for 1 hour and 15 minutes, or until 165°F is reached internally.
6. Before slicing, let the chicken ten minutes to rest.

Nutritional Value (per serving):

Calories: 350, Fat: 22g, Protein: 35g, Carbohydrates: 2g, Fiber: 1g, Net Carbs: 1g

Keto Chicken Fajita Bowl

This keto-friendly fajita dish has grilled chicken pieces served over a bed of sautéed bell peppers and onions, topped with creamy avocado and a dollop of sour cream. It's a tasty and low-carb alternative to classic fajitas.

Prep Time: 15 minutes | Cook Time: 20 minutes | Total Time: 35 minutes | Serving Size: 4 servings

Ingredients:

- 1 pound chicken breast, cut into strips
- 1 red bell pepper, sliced
- 1 green bell pepper, sliced
- 1 onion, sliced
- 1 tbsp olive oil
- 1 tsp chili powder
- 1 tsp cumin
- 1 tsp paprika
- 1 avocado, sliced
- ½ cup sour cream
- Salt and pepper to taste

Method of Preparation:

1. In a big pan, warm up the olive oil over medium heat.
2. Add salt, pepper, paprika, cumin, and chili powder to the chicken strips for seasoning.
3. Cook for five to seven minutes, or until cooked through.
4. Remove the chicken and leave aside. In the same pan, sauté the bell peppers and onion until soft.
5. Divide the peppers and onions among the serving dishes. Top with chicken pieces, avocado slices, and a dollop of sour cream.

Nutritional Value (per serving):

Calories: 350, Fat: 22g, Protein: 30g, Carbohydrates: 8g, Fiber: 5g, Net Carbs: 3g

Bacon-Wrapped Chicken Breast

Garlic and spices are used to season tender chicken breasts that are encased in crispy bacon. This tasty, high-protein dish fits well within a ketogenic diet and tastes good with every bite.

Prep Time: 10 minutes | Cook Time: 30 minutes | Total Time: 40 minutes | Serving Size: 4 servings

Ingredients:

- 4 boneless, skinless chicken breasts
- 8 pieces of bacon
- 2 cloves garlic, minced
- 1 tbsp dried oregano
- 1 tbsp dried thyme
- Salt and pepper to taste

Method of Preparation:

1. Preheat the oven to 400°F (200°C).
2. Season each chicken breast with minced garlic, oregano, thyme, salt, and pepper.
3. Using toothpicks if necessary, wrap two strips of bacon around each chicken breast.
4. Place the wrapped chicken breasts on a baking sheet lined with parchment paper.
5. Bake for 25-30 minutes, or until the chicken reaches an internal temperature of 165°F and the bacon is crispy.

Nutritional Value (per serving):

Calories: 400, Fat: 30g, Protein: 30g, Carbohydrates: 2g, Fiber: 0g, Net Carbs: 2g

Keto Chicken Piccata

Keto Chicken Piccata contains pan-fried chicken breasts covered in a zesty lemon butter sauce with capers. This recipe is light but tasty, appropriate for a keto diet while giving a typical Italian taste.

Prep Time: 10 minutes | Cook Time: 20 minutes | Total Time: 30 minutes | Serving Size: 4 servings

Ingredients:

- 4 boneless, skinless chicken breasts
- 1/4 cup almond flour
- 2 tbsp olive oil
- 1/4 cup unsalted butter
- 1/4 cup fresh lemon juice
- 1/4 cup chicken broth
- 2 tbsp capers, drained
- 2 cloves garlic, minced
- Salt and pepper to taste
- Fresh parsley, chopped (for garnish)

Method of Preparation:

1. Flatten each chicken breast to an equal thickness and season with salt and pepper. Dredge in almond flour.
2. In a pan set over medium heat, warm the olive oil. Cook chicken breasts for 4-5 minutes on each side, or until golden brown and cooked through. Remove from skillet and put aside.

3. Using the same skillet, heat butter over medium heat until it melts. Then, put in the garlic and cook it until it becomes fragrant, which should take about 1 minute.
4. Stir in lemon juice, chicken broth, and capers. Cook for 2-3 minutes, allowing the sauce to decrease somewhat.
5. Return the chicken to the skillet and ladle sauce over the top. Cook for an additional 2 minutes.
6. Garnish with fresh parsley before serving.

Nutritional Value (per serving):

Calories: 350, Fat: 24g, Protein: 30g, Carbohydrates: 5g, Fiber: 1g

Net Carbs: 4g

Thai Coconut Curry Chicken

Thai Coconut Curry Chicken includes succulent chicken thighs stewed in a thick and creamy coconut curry sauce seasoned with traditional Thai spices. When served alongside cauliflower rice, it makes for a delicious and satisfying keto-friendly dinner.

Prep Time: 15 minutes | Cook Time: 25 minutes | Total Time: 40 minutes | Serving Size: 4 servings

Ingredients:

- 1.5 lbs of boneless, skinless chicken thighs, chopped into pieces
- 1 can (14 oz) coconut milk
- 2 tbsp red curry paste
- 1 tbsp fish sauce
- 1 tbsp lime juice
- 1 tbsp olive oil
- 1 bell pepper, sliced
- 1 cup snap peas
- 2 cloves garlic, minced
- 1 tbsp fresh ginger, minced
- 1/4 cup fresh cilantro, chopped (for garnish)
- Salt to taste

Method of Preparation:

1. Warm olive oil in a large pan over medium heat. Cook chicken thighs until they're browned on all sides, about 5-7 minutes.
2. Add garlic and ginger, cooking briefly until fragrant.
3. Stir in curry paste and cook for another minute.
4. Pour in coconut milk, fish sauce, and lime juice, then stir to combine.
5. Add bell pepper and snap peas. Simmer for 15-20 minutes, or until the chicken is cooked and the vegetables are tender.
6. Garnish with fresh cilantro before serving with cauliflower rice.

Nutritional Value (per serving):

Calories: 400, Fat: 30g, Protein: 25g, Carbohydrates: 10g, Fiber: 4g, Net Carbs: 6g

Keto Chicken Tenders

Keto Chicken Tenders are crispy and tasty, covered in a blend of almond flour and Parmesan cheese. They're ideal for dipping into keto-friendly ketchup or ranch dressing.

Prep Time: 15 minutes | Cook Time: 20 minutes | Total Time: 35 minutes | Serving Size: 4 servings

Ingredients:

- 1 pound chicken tenders
- 1 cup almond flour
- 1/2 cup grated Parmesan cheese
- 2 big eggs
- 1/2 tsp garlic powder
- 1/2 tsp paprika
- Salt and pepper to taste
- Olive oil spray

Method of Preparation:

1. Turn on your oven and set it to 400°F (200°C). Get a baking sheet ready and place parchment paper on it.
2. In a separate small bowl, mix together almond flour, Parmesan cheese, garlic powder, paprika, salt, and pepper.
3. In another dish, beat eggs.
4. Dip each chicken tender into the egg, then coat with the almond flour mixture.
5. Place the coated tenders on the baking sheet that has been prepared, then generously mist with olive oil.
6. Bake, rotating halfway through, for fifteen to twenty minutes, or until golden brown and cooked through.

Nutritional Value (per serving):

Calories: 350, Fat: 22g, Protein: 30g, Carbohydrates: 8g, Fiber: 3g, Net Carbs: 5g

Tuscan Garlic Chicken

Delicious chicken breasts are cooked in a creamy sauce with sun-dried tomatoes, spinach, garlic, and heavy cream in Tuscan Garlic Chicken. It's a hearty, substantial dinner with classic Italian flavors.

Prep Time: 10 minutes | Cook Time: 20 minutes | Total Time: 30 minutes | Serving Size: 4 servings

Ingredients:

- 4 boneless, skinless chicken breasts
- 2 tbsp olive oil
- 4 cloves garlic, minced
- 1/2 cup sun-dried tomatoes, chopped
- 1 cup fresh spinach
- 1 cup heavy cream
- 1/4 cup grated Parmesan cheese
- 1/2 tsp dried basil
- Salt and pepper to taste

Method of Preparation:

1. In a big pan, warm up the olive oil over medium heat. Season chicken breasts with salt and pepper and fry for 5-7 minutes on each side or until golden brown and cooked through. Remove from skillet and put aside.
2. Add the garlic to the same skillet and cook for about a minute, or until fragrant.
3. Stir in sun-dried tomatoes and simmer for 2 minutes.
4. Add heavy cream and bring to a boil. Mix in Parmesan cheese and basil, and continue to simmer until the sauce gets a bit thicker.
5. Put the chicken back into the skillet and add the spinach. Cook for an additional 2 minutes, or until the spinach wilts and the chicken is fully cooked.

Nutritional Value (per serving):

Calories: 400, Fat: 30g, Protein: 30g, Carbohydrates: 7g, Fiber: 2g, Net Carbs: 5g

Chicken Bacon Ranch Skillet

Chicken Bacon Ranch Skillet is a filling and savory keto dish containing grilled chicken cooked with crispy bacon, ranch dressing, and cheddar cheese. It's a tasty dinner that's simple to make.

Prep Time: 10 minutes | Cook Time: 20 minutes | Total Time: 30 minutes | Serving Size: 4 servings

---

Ingredients:

- 1 pound chicken breast, dice
- 6 pieces of bacon, diced
- 1 packet (1 ounce) ranch seasoning mix
- 1 cup shredded cheddar cheese
- 2 tbsp olive oil
- Salt and pepper to taste

Method of Preparation:

1. In a big pan, warm up the olive oil over medium heat. Add diced chicken and sauté until browned and cooked through, approximately 8-10 minutes. Remove from skillet and put aside.
2. In the same skillet, fry diced bacon until crispy. Take the bacon out and place it on paper towels to absorb excess oil.
3. Return the chicken to the pan and sprinkle with ranch seasoning. Stir to coat.
4. Top with shredded cheddar cheese and heat for 2-3 minutes, or until the cheese has melted.
5. Sprinkle with crispy bacon before serving.

Nutritional Value (per serving):

Calories: 400, Fat: 30g, Protein: 30g, Carbohydrates: 5g, Fiber: 1g, Net Carbs: 4g

Chapter 8. Seafood

Garlic Butter Shrimp

Garlic Butter Shrimp is a tasty and quick-to-make meal with delicate shrimp cooked in a creamy garlic butter sauce. Perfect for a low-carb, high-fat lunch, this dish is both filling and tasty.

Prep Time: 10 minutes | Cooking Time: 8 minutes | Total Time: 18 minutes | Serving Size: 4 servings

Ingredients:

- 1 lb big shrimp, peeled and deveined
- 4 tbsp unsalted butter
- 4 cloves garlic, minced
- 1/4 cup fresh parsley, chopped
- 1/2 tsp paprika
- 1/4 tsp red pepper flakes (optional)
- Salt and pepper to taste
- Lemon wedges for serving

Method of Preparation:

1. In a big pan over medium heat, melt the butter.
2. Add minced garlic and sauté until fragrant, approximately 1 minute.
3. Add shrimp, paprika, and red pepper flakes. Cook until shrimp become pink and opaque, approximately 3-4 minutes on each side.
4. Season with salt and pepper, and mix in chopped parsley.
5. Serve immediately with lemon wedges.

Nutritional Value (per serving):

Calories: 220, Fat: 15g, Protein: 20g, Carbohydrates: 2g, Fiber: 1g, Net Carbs: 1g

Lemon Herb Grilled Salmon

Lemon Herb Grilled Salmon is a simple but exquisite meal containing salmon fillets marinated in lemon juice and herbs, then grilled to perfection. It's light, delicious, and suitable for a keto diet.

Prep Time: 15 minutes | Marinating Time: 30 minutes | Cooking Time: 10 minutes | Total Time: 55 minutes | Serving Size: 4 servings

Ingredients:

- 4 salmon fillets (6 oz each)
- 2 tbsp olive oil
- Juice of 1 lemon
- 2 cloves garlic, minced
- 1 tbsp fresh dill, diced (or 1 tsp dried dill)
- 1 tbsp fresh parsley, chopped
- Salt and pepper to taste

Method of Preparation:

1. In a bowl, mix together olive oil, lemon juice, garlic, dill, parsley, salt, and pepper.

2. Place salmon fillets in a resealable bag or plate and pour marinade over them. Refrigerate for 30 minutes.
3. Preheat the grill to medium-high heat.
4. Grill salmon for approximately 4-5 minutes on each side, or until fish is cooked through and flakes readily with a fork.
5. Serve hot.

Nutritional Value (per serving):

Calories: 290, Fat: 20g, Protein: 25g, Carbohydrates: 2g, Fiber: 1g, Net Carbs: 1g

Coconut Curry Fish

Coconut Curry Fish contains flaky white fish cooked in a creamy coconut curry sauce. It's a warm, low-carb dish that's rich in taste and appropriate for the ketogenic diet.

Prep Time: 10 minutes | Cooking Time: 20 minutes | Total Time: 30 minutes | Serving Size: 4 servings

Ingredients:

- One Pound of white fish fillets (e.g., cod or tilapia)
- 1 tbsp coconut oil
- 1 small onion, chopped
- 2 cloves garlic, minced
- 1 tbsp fresh ginger, minced
- 1 can (14 oz) coconut milk
- 2 tbsp red curry paste
- 1 tbsp fish sauce
- 1 cup spinach leaves
- Salt and pepper to taste
- Fresh cilantro for garnish

Method of Preparation:

1. In a big pan set over medium heat, warm up the coconut oil. Add onion, garlic, and ginger; sauté until onion is transparent.
2. Stir in red curry paste and simmer for 1-2 minutes.
3. Add coconut milk and fish sauce, bringing to a boil.
4. Add fish fillets and simmer for approximately 10 minutes or until fish flakes easily.
5. Stir in spinach and simmer until wilted.
6. Season with salt and pepper, then sprinkle with fresh cilantro before serving.

Nutritional Value (per serving):

Calories: 280, Fat: 18g, Protein: 22g, Carbohydrates: 5g, Fiber: 2g, Net Carbs: 3g

Baked Crab Cakes with Avocado Salsa

Baked Crab Cakes with Avocado Salsa give a tasty and keto-friendly take on a popular meal. These crab cakes are baked for a healthier choice and topped with fresh avocado salsa.

Prep Time: 20 minutes | Cooking Time: 20 minutes | Total Time: 40 minutes | Serving Size: 4 servings

Ingredients:

For Crab Cakes:

- 1 pound lump crab meat
- 1/2 cup almond flour
- 1 egg, beaten
- 1/4 cup mayonnaise
- 1 tbsp Dijon mustard
- 1 tbsp fresh parsley, chopped
- 1 tsp Old Bay seasoning
- Salt and pepper to taste

For Avocado Salsa:

- 1 ripe avocado, chopped
- 1 small tomato, chopped
- 1/4 cup red onion, finely chopped
- 1 tbsp fresh cilantro, chopped
- Juice of 1 lime
- Salt and pepper to taste

Method of Preparation:

1. Preheat oven to 375°F (190°C). Line a baking sheet with parchment paper to prepare it.
2. In a bowl, mix crab meat, almond flour, egg, mayonnaise, Dijon mustard, parsley, Old Bay seasoning, salt, and pepper.
3. Form the mixture into 8 cakes and put them on the prepared baking sheet.
4. Bake for fifteen to twenty minutes, or until the cakes are cooked through and have a golden brown color.
5. For the salsa, mix avocado, tomato, red onion, cilantro, lime juice, salt, and pepper in a bowl.
6. Place avocado salsa over the crab cakes and serve.

Nutritional Value (per serving):

Calories: 320, Fat: 23g, Protein: 22g, Carbohydrates: 8g, Fiber: 4g, Net Carbs: 4g

Keto Tuna Salad

Keto Tuna Salad is a traditional, creamy salad prepared with tuna, mayonnaise, and crisp veggies. It's a terrific low-carb lunch or snack choice, filled with protein and healthy fats.

Prep Time: 10 minutes | Cooking Time: 0 minutes | Total Time: 10 minutes | Serving Size: 4 servings

Ingredients:

- 2 cans (5 oz each) tuna, drained
- 1/4 cup mayonnaise
- 1 tbsp Dijon mustard
- 1/4 cup celery, chopped
- 1/4 cup red onion, finely chopped
- 1 tbsp fresh parsley, chopped
- Salt and pepper to taste

Method of Preparation:

1. In a bowl, whisk together tuna, mayonnaise, Dijon mustard, celery, red onion, and parsley.
2. Season with salt and pepper to taste.
3. Serve refrigerated or at room temperature.

Nutritional Value (per serving):

Calories: 240, Fat: 18g, Protein: 18g, Carbohydrates: 2g, Fiber: 1g, Net Carbs: 1g

Creamy Garlic Parmesan Scallops

Creamy Garlic Parmesan Scallops are delicate scallops served in a thick and creamy garlic Parmesan sauce. This keto-friendly recipe is fast to make and excellent for a low-carb, high-fat supper.

Prep Time: 10 minutes | Cooking Time: 10 minutes | Total Time: 20 minutes | Serving Size: 4 servings

Ingredients:

- 1 pound sea scallops, patted dry
- 2 tbsp olive oil
- 4 cloves garlic, minced
- 1 cup heavy cream
- 1/2 cup grated Parmesan cheese
- 1/4 cup fresh parsley, chopped
- Salt and pepper to taste

Method of Preparation:

1. In a spacious pan, warm up the olive oil over medium-high heat.
2. Add scallops and heat for 2-3 minutes on each side, until golden brown and cooked through. Take the scallops out of the pan and put them to the side.
3. In the same pan, add minced garlic and sauté until fragrant, approximately 1 minute.
4. Pour in heavy cream and bring to a boil. Mix in Parmesan cheese until it's melted and the sauce becomes thicker.
5. Put the scallops back into the pan and toss them around to cover them in the sauce.
6. Season with salt, pepper, and chopped parsley before serving.

Nutritional Value (per serving):

Calories: 350, Fat: 30g, Protein: 22g, Carbohydrates: 5g, Fiber: 1g, Net Carbs: 4g

Spicy Baked Cod with Lime

Spicy Baked Cod with Lime is a tasty, low-carb meal with cod fillets baked with a spicy rub and a zesty lime sauce. It's an easy, nutritious substitute that works well for a ketogenic diet.

Prep Time: 10 minutes | Cooking Time: 15 minutes | Total Time: 25 minutes | Serving Size: 4 servings

Ingredients:

- 4 cod fillets (6 oz each)
- 2 tbsp olive oil
- 1 tsp smoked paprika
- 1/2 tsp cayenne pepper
- 1/2 tsp garlic powder
- 1/2 tsp onion powder
- 1/2 tsp dried oregano
- Juice of 1 lime
- Salt and pepper to taste
- Lime wedges for serving

Method of Preparation:

1. Preheat oven to 400°F (200°C). Line a baking sheet with parchment paper to prepare it.
2. In a small bowl, whisk together paprika, cayenne pepper, garlic powder, onion powder, oregano, salt, and pepper.
3. Rub fish fillets with olive oil, then sprinkle with the spice mixture.
4. Put the fillets on the baking sheet you prepared earlier and bake them for 12-15 minutes, or until the fish easily flakes apart when you poke it with a fork.
5. Drizzle with lime juice before serving and garnish with lime wedges.

Nutritional Value (per serving):

Calories: 220, Fat: 12g, Protein: 25g, Carbohydrates: 1g, Fiber: 0g, Net Carbs: 1g

Shrimp and Avocado Salad

Shrimp & Avocado Salad blends juicy shrimp with creamy avocado and fresh veggies for a tasty and healthy keto-friendly dinner. It's light but satisfying, making it a terrific option for lunch or supper.

Prep Time: 15 minutes | Cooking Time: 5 minutes | Total Time: 20 minutes | Serving Size: 4 servings

Ingredients:

- 1 lb big shrimp, peeled and deveined
- 2 tbsp olive oil
- 1 tsp paprika
- 1/2 tsp garlic powder
- 1/2 tsp onion powder
- 1 avocado, diced
- 2 cups mixed salad greens
- 1/2 cup cherry tomatoes, halved
- 1/4 cup red onion, thinly sliced
- 2 tbsp lemon juice
- Salt and pepper to taste

Method of Preparation:

1. Warm up some olive oil in a pan using medium-high heat. Add shrimp and season with paprika, garlic powder, and onion powder.
2. Cook the shrimp for 2-3 minutes per side, or until they turn pink and become opaque. Remove from heat and let cool.
3. In a large bowl, mix salad greens, cherry tomatoes, red onion, and avocado.
4. Add cooked shrimp and sprinkle with lemon juice.
5. Toss gently to incorporate and season with salt and pepper before serving.

Nutritional Value (per serving):

Calories: 280, Fat: 18g, Protein: 22g, Carbohydrates: 8g, Fiber: 5g, Net Carbs: 3g

Lemon Dill Baked Halibut

Lemon dill-cooked Halibut includes delicious halibut fillets cooked with a fresh lemon and dill flavor. This keto-friendly recipe is easy to make and has a light, zesty taste that's excellent for any meal.

Prep Time: 10 minutes | Cooking Time: 15 minutes | Total Time: 25 minutes | Serving Size: 4 servings

---

Ingredients:

- 4 halibut fillets (6 oz each)
- 2 tbsp olive oil
- Juice of 1 lemon
- 1 tbsp fresh dill, chopped
- 2 cloves garlic, minced
- Salt and pepper to taste
- Lemon wedges for serving

Method of Preparation:

1. Preheat oven to 375°F (190°C). Place a sheet of parchment paper inside a baking dish.
2. Place halibut fillets in the prepared baking dish and brush with olive oil.
3. Sprinkle with lemon juice, chopped dill, and minced garlic.
4. Season with salt and pepper.
5. Bake for 12-15 minutes, or until fish is cooked through and flakes readily with a fork.
6. Serve with lemon wedges.

Nutritional Value (per serving):

Calories: 240, Fat: 15g, Protein: 22g, Carbohydrates: 2g, Fiber: 0g, Net Carbs: 2g

Garlic Herb Mussels

Garlic Herb Mussels are a tasty and keto-friendly seafood meal with mussels boiled in a flavorful garlic herb broth. This low-carb dish is excellent for a light but tasty evening.

Prep Time: 10 minutes | Cooking Time: 15 minutes | Total Time: 25 minutes | Serving Size: 4 servings

Ingredients:

- 2 pounds fresh mussels, washed and debearded
- 2 tbsp olive oil
- 4 cloves garlic, minced
- 1/4 cup white wine (optional, may use chicken broth as an alternative)
- 1/4 cup fresh parsley, chopped
- 1 tsp dried thyme
- Salt and pepper to taste
- Lemon wedges for serving

Method of Preparation:

1. Heat olive oil in a big saucepan over medium heat. Add minced garlic and sauté until fragrant, approximately 1 minute.
2. Pour in white wine or chicken broth and bring to a boil.
3. Add mussels and cover the pot. Steam the mussels until they open, which should take about 5-7 minutes.
4. Stir in parsley, thyme, salt, and pepper.
5. Discard any mussels that haven't opened. Serve with lemon wedges.

Nutritional Value (per serving):

Calories: 200, Fat: 8g, Protein: 25g, Carbohydrates: 4g, Fiber: 1g, Net Carbs: 3g

Salmon Patties with Dill Sauce

Samon Patties with Dill Sauce is a tasty and keto-friendly dinner that blends delicate fish with fresh dill. The patties are crisp on the exterior and soft within, topped with a creamy dill sauce for a delightful dinner.

Prep Time: 15 minutes | Cooking Time: 10 minutes | Total Time: 25 minutes | Serving Size: 4 servings

Ingredients:

- One can (14.75 ounce) of salmon, drained and flaked
- 1/4 cup almond flour
- 1/4 cup grated Parmesan cheese
- 1 egg, beaten
- 2 tbsp fresh dill, chopped
- 1/4 cup finely chopped onion
- 2 cloves garlic, minced
- Salt and pepper to taste
- 2 tbsp olive oil
- For the Dill Sauce:
- 1/2 cup sour cream
- 2 tbsp fresh dill, chopped
- 1 tbsp lemon juice
- Salt and pepper to taste

Method of Preparation:

1. In a large bowl, add flaked salmon, almond flour, Parmesan cheese, beaten egg, fresh dill, diced onion, and minced garlic. Mix until completely blended.
2. Form the mixture into 8 tiny patties.
3. In a pan set over medium heat, warm the olive oil. Cook patties for 3-4 minutes on each side, until golden brown and cooked through.
4. For the dill sauce, whisk sour cream, minced dill, lemon juice, salt, and pepper in a small bowl.
5. Serve patties with dill sauce.

Nutritional Value (per serving):

Calories: 270, Fat: 20g, Protein: 20g, Carbohydrates: 4g, Fiber: 1g, Net Carbs: 3g

Coconut Lime Shrimp

Coconut Lime Shrimp includes luscious shrimp served in a creamy coconut sauce with a zesty lime flavor. This meal is fast to make and delivers a lovely combination of tropical tastes.

Prep Time: 10 minutes | Cooking Time: 10 minutes | Total Time: 20 minutes | Serving Size: 4 servings

Ingredients:

- 1 lb big shrimp, peeled and deveined
- 1 tbsp coconut oil
- 1 can (14 oz) full-fat coconut milk
- Juice of 2 limes
- 2 cloves garlic, minced
- 1 tsp ginger, grated
- 1/2 tsp cayenne pepper (optional)
- Salt and pepper to taste
- Fresh cilantro for garnish

Method of Preparation:

1. Warm up some coconut oil in a big pan using medium-high heat. Add shrimp and cook for 2-3 minutes each side until pink and opaque. Remove shrimp and leave aside.
2. In the same skillet, add minced garlic and grated ginger. Cook for 1 minute until aromatic.
3. Pour in coconut milk and lime juice. Bring to a boil and cook for 2-3 minutes until the sauce thickens slightly.
4. Return shrimp to the pan and toss to coat in the sauce.
5. Season with cayenne pepper (if using), salt, and pepper. Garnish with fresh cilantro before serving.

Nutritional Value (per serving):

Calories: 290, Fat: 20g, Protein: 20g, Carbohydrates: 7g, Fiber: 2g, Net Carbs: 5g

Keto Shrimp Scampi with Zucchini Noodles

Keto Shrimp Scampi with Zucchini Noodles is a low-carb take on the traditional shrimp scampi. Juicy shrimp are sautéed in a garlic butter sauce and served over spiralized zucchini noodles for a light and tasty supper.

Prep Time: 15 minutes | Cooking Time: 10 minutes | Total Time: 25 minutes | Serving Size: 4 servings

Ingredients:

- 1 lb big shrimp, peeled and deveined
- 2 tbsp butter
- 4 cloves garlic, minced
- 1/4 cup dry white wine or chicken broth
- Juice of 1 lemon
- 1/4 cup chopped parsley
- 4 cups zucchini noodles
- Salt and pepper to taste

Method of Preparation:

1. Heat butter in a large skillet over medium-high heat. Add minced garlic and sauté until fragrant, approximately 1 minute.
2. Add shrimp and cook for 2-3 minutes each side until pink and opaque. Take the shrimp out of the pan and set them aside.
3. Pour in white wine or chicken broth and lemon juice. Bring to a boil and cook for 2-3 minutes until the sauce reduces somewhat.
4. Add zucchini noodles to the pan and simmer for 2-3 minutes until cooked.
5. Return shrimp to the skillet and stir everything to incorporate. Season with salt, pepper, and chopped parsley before serving.

Nutritional Value (per serving):

Calories: 270, Fat: 17g, Protein: 23g, Carbohydrates: 7g, Fiber: 2g, Net Carbs: 5g

Crispy Baked Fish Tenders

Crispy Baked Fish Tenders are a healthy, keto-friendly alternative to fried fish sticks. Coated in a crispy almond flour crust and baked till brown, these tenders are excellent for a low-carb dinner or snack.

Prep Time: 15 minutes | Cooking Time: 15 minutes | Total Time: 30 minutes | Serving Size: 4 servings

Ingredients:

- 1 lb white fish fillets (such as cod or tilapia), cut into pieces
- 1 cup almond flour
- 1/2 cup grated Parmesan cheese
- 2 eggs, beaten
- 1 tsp paprika
- 1/2 tsp garlic powder
- Salt and pepper to taste
- Cooking spray

Method of Preparation:

1. Preheat oven to 400°F (200°C). Prepare a baking sheet by placing parchment paper on it and then lightly coating it with cooking spray.
2. In a small bowl, combine almond flour, Parmesan cheese, paprika, garlic powder, salt, and pepper.
3. Dip each fish strip into the beaten eggs, then coat with the almond flour mixture.
4. Place greased fish strips on the prepared baking sheet.
5. Bake for 12-15 minutes, or until fish is cooked through and the coating is golden brown and crispy.

Nutritional Value (per serving):

Calories: 250, Fat: 16g, Protein: 22g, Carbohydrates: 5g, Fiber: 2g, Net Carbs: 3g

Seafood Stuffed Bell Peppers

Seafood Stuffed Bell Peppers are a rich and hearty meal with bell peppers packed with a savory blend of seafood, cheese, and seasonings. This keto-friendly dish is excellent for a nutritious supper.

Prep Time: 20 minutes | Cooking Time: 30 minutes | Total Time: 50 minutes | Serving Size: 4 servings

---

Ingredients:

- 4 big bell peppers, tops cut off and seeds removed
- 1/2-pound shrimp, peeled and cut
- 1/2-pound crab meat
- 1/2 cup cream cheese, softened
- 1/4 cup mayonnaise
- 1/2 cup shredded cheddar cheese
- 1/4 cup chopped green onions
- 1 tsp Old Bay seasoning
- Salt and pepper to taste

Method of Preparation:

1. Preheat oven to 375°F (190°C). Place bell peppers in a baking dish.
2. In a large bowl, add shrimp, crab meat, cream cheese, mayonnaise, cheddar cheese, green onions, Old Bay seasoning, salt, and pepper.
3. Stuff each bell pepper with the seafood mixture.
4. Bake for 30 minutes, or until the peppers are soft and the mixture is heated through.
5. Serve warm.

Nutritional Value (per serving):

Calories: 300, Fat: 22g, Protein: 22g, Carbohydrates: 9g, Fiber: 3g, Net Carbs: 6g

Chapter 9. Plant-based Proteins

Spicy Tofu Stir-Fry

Spicy Tofu Stir-Fry is a tasty and comforting recipe that blends tofu with a mixture of low-carb veggies and a spicy sauce. It's excellent for a fast-evening supper or as a healthy lunch choice.

Prep Time: 15 minutes | Cooking Time: 15 minutes | Total Time: 30 minutes | Serving Size: 2 servings

Ingredients:

- One block (14 ounce) of firm tofu, drained and cubed
- 1 tbsp olive oil
- 1 red bell pepper, sliced
- 1 cup broccoli florets
- 1 cup snap peas
- 2 cloves garlic, minced
- 1 tbsp fresh ginger, minced
- 2 tbsp soy sauce (or tamari for gluten-free)
- 1 tbsp sriracha sauce (modify to taste)
- 1 tbsp rice vinegar
- 1 tsp sesame oil
- 1 tbsp sesame seeds (optional)
- Green onions for garnish (optional)

Method of Preparation:

1. Preheat the oven to 400°F (200°C). Line a baking sheet with parchment paper to prepare it.
2. Place the tofu cubes on the baking pan and bake for 20 minutes, turning halfway through until golden and crispy.
3. Heat olive oil in a large pan or wok over medium-high heat.
4. Add garlic and ginger, stirring for 30 seconds until aromatic.
5. Add bell pepper, broccoli, and snap peas to the skillet. Stir-fry for 5-7 minutes until veggies are tender-crisp.
6. In a small bowl, combine soy sauce, sriracha, rice vinegar, and sesame oil. Pour over the veggies.
7. Put the baked tofu into the pan, making sure to mix everything well so it's all coated.
8. Garnish with sesame seeds and green onions if preferred. Serve immediately.

Nutritional Value (per serving):

Calories: 280, Protein: 15g, Fat: 20g, Carbohydrates: 16g, Fiber: 5g, Net Carbs: 11g

Crispy Baked Tempeh

Crispy Baked Tempeh is a crispy, protein-packed snack or dinner component that works nicely with a number of cuisines. Seasoned with herbs and spices, it's a simple and tasty way to consume tempeh.

Prep Time: 10 minutes | Cooking Time: 25 minutes | Total Time: 35 minutes | Serving Size: 2 servings

Ingredients:

- One package (8 ounces) tempeh, cut into thin strips
- 2 tbsp olive oil
- 1 tsp smoked paprika
- 1/2 tsp garlic powder
- 1/2 tsp onion powder
- 1/2 tsp dried oregano
- Salt and pepper to taste

Method of Preparation:

1. Preheat the oven to 400°F (200°C). Line a baking sheet with parchment paper to prepare it.
2. In a small bowl, combine olive oil, smoked paprika, garlic powder, onion powder, dried oregano, salt, and pepper.
3. Toss the tempeh strips in the olive oil mixture until evenly coated.
4. Lay out the tempeh strips in a single layer on the baking sheet you've already prepared. Bake for 20-25 minutes, making sure to turn them over halfway through, until they become brown and crispy.
5. Serve warm as a snack or side dish

Nutritional Value (per serving):

Calories: 210, Protein: 14g, Fat: 14g, Carbohydrates: 12g, Fiber: 6g, Net Carbs: 6g

Avocado and Chickpea Salad

Avocado and Chickpea Salad is a delicious and creamy salad that's excellent for a light lunch or side. The combination of mashed chickpeas and ripe avocado creates a pleasing texture and taste.

Prep Time: 10 minutes | Cooking Time: None | Total Time: 10 minutes | Serving Size: 2 servings

Ingredients:

- One can (15 ounce) of chickpeas, drained and rinsed
- 1 ripe avocado, chopped
- 1/4 cup red onion, finely chopped
- 1/4 cup fresh parsley, chopped
- 2 tbsp lemon juice
- 1 tbsp olive oil
- Salt and pepper to taste

Method of Preparation:

1. In a large bowl, mash half of the chickpeas using a fork or potato masher.
2. Put in the rest of the whole chickpeas, diced avocado, red onion, and parsley.
3. Lightly pour lemon juice and olive oil over the mixture, then add salt and pepper to taste.
4. Gently mix everything until thoroughly blended.
5. You can enjoy it right away, or store it in the refrigerator until you're ready to have it.

Nutritional Value (per serving):

Calories: 280, Protein: 9g, Fat: 18g, Carbohydrates: 23g, Fiber: 8g, Net Carbs: 15g

Cauliflower Rice with Black Bean Bowl

Cauliflower Rice & Black Bean Bowl is a filling and delicious recipe that mixes cauliflower rice with black beans, avocado, and a tart lime sauce. It's a low-carb, nutrient-dense supper.

Prep Time: 15 minutes | Cooking Time: 10 minutes | Total Time: 25 minutes | Serving Size: 2 servings

Ingredients:

- 1 head of cauliflower, shredded into rice-sized pieces
- One cup canned of black beans, drained and rinsed
- 1 ripe avocado, sliced
- 1/2 cup cherry tomatoes, halved
- 1/4 cup cilantro, chopped
- Juice of 1 lime
- 1 tbsp olive oil
- Salt and pepper to taste

Method of Preparation:

1. Warm up some olive oil in a large pan over medium heat.
2. Then, put in the cauliflower rice and let it cook for 5-7 minutes, stirring it often until it's done.

3. In a large bowl, mix cooked cauliflower rice, black beans, avocado, cherry tomatoes, and cilantro.
4. Lightly pour lime juice over the dish and add salt and pepper as desired. Gently mix everything together.
5. Serve heated or at room temperature.

Nutritional Value (per serving):

Calories: 260, Protein: 9g, Fat: 14g, Carbohydrates: 26g, Fiber: 10g, Net Carbs: 16g

Stuffed Portobello Mushrooms

Stuffed Portobello Mushrooms are a tasty and gratifying recipe that comprises huge mushroom caps packed with a delectable blend of spinach, almond flour, and nutritional yeast. Perfect as a main course or a generous side dish.

Prep Time: 15 minutes | Cooking Time: 20 minutes | Total Time: 35 minutes | Serving Size: 2 servings

Ingredients:

- 4 big portobello mushrooms, stems removed
- 1 cup fresh spinach, chopped
- 1/4 cup almond flour
- 1/4 cup nutritional yeast
- 2 tbsp olive oil
- 1 clove garlic, minced
- Salt and pepper to taste

Method of Preparation:

1. Preheat the oven to 375°F (190°C). Line a baking sheet with parchment paper to prepare it.
2. In a pan, warm up some olive oil over medium heat. Add garlic and cook it briefly until it releases its fragrance, which should take about a minute.
3. Add spinach to the pan and heat until wilted, approximately 2 minutes.
4. Stir in almond flour and nutritional yeast, blending thoroughly. Season with salt and pepper.
5. Spoon the spinach mixture into each portobello mushroom cap.
6. Place the filled mushrooms on the prepared baking sheet and bake for 15-20 minutes, until the mushrooms are soft and the tops are golden brown.
7. Serve warm.

Nutritional Value (per serving):

Calories: 190, Protein: 7g, Fat: 15g, Carbohydrates: 10g, Fiber: 5g, Net Carbs: 5g

Zucchini Noodles with Peanut Sauce

Zucchini Noodles with Peanut Sauce is a refreshing and creamy meal with spiralized zucchini noodles served with rich peanut sauce. It's a low-carb, tasty alternative to typical pasta recipes.

Prep Time: 15 minutes | Cooking Time: 5 minutes | Total Time: 20 minutes | Serving Size: 2 servings

---

Ingredients:

- 2 medium zucchinis, spiralized into noodles
- 1/4 cup creamy peanut butter
- Two tablespoon soy sauce (or tamari for gluten-free)
- 1 tbsp lime juice
- 1 tbsp rice vinegar
- 1 tsp grated ginger
- 1 clove garlic, minced
- 1 tbsp water (to thin sauce)
- 1 tbsp sesame seeds (optional, for garnish)
- Sliced green onions (optional, for garnish)

Method of Preparation:

1. In a small bowl, mix together peanut butter, soy sauce, lime juice, rice vinegar, ginger, garlic, and water until smooth. If needed, you can add more water to get the desired consistency.
2. Toss spiralized zucchini noodles in a large dish with the peanut sauce until fully covered.
3. Heat a non-stick pan over medium heat and add the zucchini noodles. Cook for 2-3 minutes, stirring periodically, until slightly soft.
4. Serve warm, topped with sesame seeds and green onions if preferred.

Nutritional Value (per serving):

Calories: 300, Protein: 8g, Fat: 22g, Carbohydrates: 18g, Fiber: 4g, Net Carbs: 14g

Keto Vegan Chili

Keto Vegan Chili is a powerful and tasty chili cooked with black soybeans, tomatoes, and a combination of spices. It's excellent for a meaty, low-carb lunch that fits within a hyper ketosis diet.

Prep Time: 10 minutes | Cooking Time: 30 minutes | Total Time: 40 minutes | Serving Size: 4 servings

---

Ingredients:

- 1 tbsp olive oil
- 1 onion, chopped
- 2 cloves garlic, minced
- 1 red bell pepper, chopped
- 1 can (15 oz) chopped tomatoes
- One can (15 ounce) of black soybeans, drained and rinsed
- 1 tbsp chili powder
- 1 tsp cumin

- 1/2 tsp smoked paprika
- 1/2 tsp oregano
- Salt and pepper to taste
- 1 cup vegetable broth
- Fresh cilantro, chopped (for garnish)

Method of Preparation:

1. In a spacious saucepan, heat the olive oil over medium heat. Put in the onion and cook until it softens, which should take about 5 minutes.
2. Next, add the garlic and red bell pepper, and continue cooking for another 2 minutes.
3. Stir in chopped tomatoes, black soybeans, chili powder, cumin, smoked paprika, oregano, salt, and pepper.
4. Add the vegetable broth and heat until it boils.
5. Cook for 20-25 minutes, stirring periodically, until flavors are merged and chili has thickened.
6. Garnish with fresh cilantro before serving.

Nutritional Value (per serving):

Calories: 250, Protein: 10g, Fat: 10g, Carbohydrates: 20g, Fiber: 7g, Net Carbs: 13g

Almond Flour Crusted Tofu Nuggets

Almond Flour Crusted Tofu Nuggets are crispy and delicious, delivering a crunchy texture that is excellent as a snack or main meal. Coated in almond flour and cooked to perfection, these nuggets are a wonderful low-carb, high-protein alternative.

Prep Time: 10 minutes | Cooking Time: 25 minutes | Total Time: 35 minutes | Serving Size: 2 servings

Ingredients:

- One block (14 ounce) of firm tofu, drained and cubed
- 1 cup almond flour
- 1/2 cup grated Parmesan cheese
- 1/2 tsp garlic powder
- 1/2 tsp paprika
- 1/2 tsp salt
- 1/4 tsp black pepper
- 1 big egg, beaten

Method of Preparation:

1. Preheat the oven to 400°F (200°C). Line a baking sheet with parchment paper to prepare it.
2. In a small bowl, combine almond flour, Parmesan cheese, garlic powder, paprika, salt, and pepper.
3. Dip each tofu cube into the beaten egg, then coat with the almond flour mixture, pressing gently to adhere.
4. Place covered tofu cubes on the prepared baking sheet.
5. Bake the nuggets for twenty to twenty-five minutes, rotating them halfway through, or until they are crispy and golden.

6. Serve heated with your favorite dipping sauce.

Nutritional Value (per serving):

Calories: 300, Protein: 20g, Fat: 22g, Carbohydrates: 12g, Fiber: 5g, Net Carbs: 7g

Coconut Curry Cauliflower Steaks

Coconut Curry Cauliflower Steaks are thick slices of cauliflower marinated in a creamy coconut curry sauce and then roasted till soft and fragrant. This meal creates a tasty and fulfilling plant-based main course.

Prep Time: 10 minutes | Cooking Time: 30 minutes | Total Time: 40 minutes | Serving Size: 2 servings

Ingredients:

- 1 full head of cauliflower, sliced into 1/2-inch-thick steaks
- 1 can (13.5 oz) coconut milk
- 2 tbsp red curry paste
- 1 tbsp lime juice
- 1 tbsp olive oil
- 1 tbsp fresh cilantro, chopped (for garnish)
- Salt and pepper to taste

Method of Preparation:

1. Preheat the oven to 425°F (220°C). Line a baking sheet with parchment paper to prepare it.
2. In a small bowl, mix together coconut milk, red curry paste, lime juice, olive oil, salt, and pepper.
3. Brush each cauliflower steak with the curry sauce, ensuring a uniform covering.
4. Place cauliflower steaks on the oven sheet and roast for 25-30 minutes, until soft and golden brown.
5. Garnish with fresh cilantro before serving.

Nutritional Value (per serving):

Calories: 270, Protein: 5g, Fat: 23g, Carbohydrates: 20g, Fiber: 6g, Net Carbs: 14g

Creamy Avocado Spinach Smoothie

Creamy Avocado Spinach Smoothie is a nutrient-dense smoothie that mixes the rich tastes of avocado with the freshness of spinach. This smoothie is excellent for a quick breakfast or a mid-day boost.

Prep Time: 5 minutes | Cooking Time: None | Total Time: 5 minutes | Serve Size: 1 serve

Ingredients:

- 1 ripe avocado
- 1 cup fresh spinach
- 1 cup unsweetened almond milk
- 1 tbsp chia seeds (optional, for extra texture)

- 1 tbsp lemon juice
- 1/2 tsp vanilla extract
- Stevia or erythritol to taste (optional)

Method of Preparation:

1. In a blender, add avocado, spinach, almond milk, chia seeds, lemon juice, and vanilla essence.
2. Blend until smooth and creamy.
3. Taste and adjust sweetness with stevia or erythritol if desired.
4. Pour into a glass and drink immediately.

Nutritional Value (per serving):

Calories: 300, Protein: 5g, Fat: 24g, Carbohydrates: 16g, Fiber: 10g, Net Carbs: 6g

Lentil and Mushroom Bolognese

Lentil and Mushroom Bolognese is a hearty, plant-based variation of the traditional Italian meat sauce. It has lentils and mushrooms cooked in a thick tomato sauce, great for combining with zucchini noodles or other low-carb pasta replacements.

Prep Time: 15 minutes | Cooking Time: 30 minutes | Total Time: 45 minutes | Serving Size: 4 servings

Ingredients:

- 1 tbsp olive oil
- 1 onion, chopped
- 2 cloves garlic, minced
- 1 cup mushrooms, finely chopped
- 1 cup dry lentils (green or brown)
- 1 can (15 oz) crushed tomatoes
- 1/2 cup vegetable broth
- 1 tbsp tomato paste
- 1 tsp dried oregano
- 1 tsp dried basil
- Salt and pepper to taste

Method of Preparation:

1. Warm up some olive oil in a spacious pan using medium heat. Add onion and simmer until softened approximately 5 minutes.
2. Add garlic and mushrooms, simmering for another 5 minutes.
3. Stir in lentils, smashed tomatoes, vegetable broth, tomato paste, oregano, basil, salt, and pepper.
4. Bring to a boil, then decrease heat and simmer for 25-30 minutes, until lentils are soft and sauce has thickened.
5. Serve over zucchini noodles or your favorite low-carb pasta replacement.

Nutritional Value (per serving):

Calories: 250, Protein: 15g, Fat: 6g, Carbohydrates: 35g, Fiber: 10g, Net Carbs: 25g

Chia Seed Pudding with Almond Butter

Chia Seed Pudding with Almond Butter is a delicious and pleasant dessert or snack. The chia seeds make a pudding-like texture, while almond butter offers a rich, nutty taste, and a few berries lend a hint of sweetness.

Prep Time: 10 minutes | Cooking Time: None | Total Time: 2 hours (for pudding to set) | Serve Size: 1 serve

Ingredients:

- 3 tbsp chia seeds
- 1 cup unsweetened almond milk
- 1 tbsp almond butter
- 1 tsp maple syrup or low-carb sweetener (optional)
- 1/2 tsp vanilla extract
- A few berries for topping (such as strawberries or blueberries)

Method of Preparation:

1. In a bowl, mix together chia seeds, almond milk, almond butter, maple syrup, and vanilla extract until completely incorporated.
2. Cover the bowl and refrigerate for at least 2 hours or overnight, enabling the chia seeds to absorb the liquid and thicken.
3. Before serving, mix the pudding and sprinkle with fresh berries.

Nutritional Value (per serving):

Calories: 250, Protein: 6g, Fat: 18g, Carbohydrates: 20g, Fiber: 8g, Net Carbs: 12g

Vegan Stuffed Bell Peppers

Vegan Stuffed Bell Peppers are bright and healthy, stuffed with a substantial blend of quinoa, black beans, and spices. They produce a full and healthful dinner that's excellent for a low-carb, plant-based diet.

Prep Time: 15 minutes | Cooking Time: 30 minutes | Total Time: 45 minutes | Serving Size: 4 servings

Ingredients:

- 4 huge bell peppers (any color)
- 1 cup cooked quinoa
- One can (15 ounce) of black beans, drained and rinsed
- 1 cup corn kernels (optional)
- 1/2 cup chopped tomatoes
- 1/2 cup diced onions
- 1 tsp chili powder
- 1/2 tsp cumin
- 1/2 tsp paprika
- Salt and pepper to taste
- 1/2 cup shredded vegan cheese (optional)

Method of Preparation:

1. Preheat oven to 375°F (190°C). Slice off the top parts of the bell peppers and clean out the seeds and white membranes from inside.

2. In a bowl, combine cooked quinoa, black beans, corn, chopped tomatoes, onions, chili powder, cumin, paprika, salt, and pepper.
3. Stuff the bell peppers with the quinoa mixture and set them in a baking tray.
4. If using, put shredded vegan cheese on top of the filled peppers.
5. Bake for 30 minutes, until the peppers are soft and the mixture is cooked through.

Nutritional Value (per serving):

Calories: 220, Protein: 10g, Fat: 4g, Carbohydrates: 38g, Fiber: 8g, Net Carbs: 30g

Broccoli and Cheddar Stuffed Mushrooms

Broccoli and Cheddar Stuffed Mushrooms are a tasty, low-carb appetizer or side dish. The mushrooms are stuffed with a cheese, and broccoli combination, giving them a delectable and gratifying alternative for a plant-based diet.

Prep Time: 10 minutes | Cooking Time: 20 minutes | Total Time: 30 minutes | Serve Size: 4 servings (approximately 2 filled mushrooms each serve)

Ingredients:

- 12 huge mushroom caps
- 1 cup finely chopped broccoli florets
- 1/2 cup shredded cheddar cheese (or vegan cheese for a plant-based alternative)
- 1/4 cup nutritional yeast
- 1 clove garlic, minced
- 1 tbsp olive oil
- Salt and pepper to taste

Method of Preparation:

1. Preheat oven to 375°F (190°C). Clean mushroom tops and remove stems.
2. Heat the olive oil in a pan over medium heat. Put in the garlic and cook it for one minute.
3. Then, add the chopped broccoli to the pan and cook until it becomes tender, which should take about five minutes.
4. In a bowl, combine cooked broccoli, cheddar cheese, nutritional yeast, salt, and pepper.
5. Fill each mushroom cap with the broccoli and cheese combination, then place them on a baking pan.
6. Bake for 15-20 minutes, until mushrooms are soft and the cheese is melted and bubbling.

Nutritional Value (per serving):

Calories: 180, Protein: 12g, Fat: 12g, Carbohydrates: 10g, Fiber: 3g, Net, Carbs: 7g

Sesame Ginger Tofu Salad

Sesame Ginger Tofu Salad is a light but substantial lunch with marinated tofu cubes, crisp veggies, and a spicy sesame ginger vinaigrette. It's a fantastic low-carb, high-protein alternative for a refreshing lunch or supper.

Prep Time: 15 minutes | Cooking Time: 10 minutes | Total Time: 25 minutes | Serving Size: 2 servings

---

Ingredients:

- One block (14 ounce) of firm tofu, drained and cubed
- 1 tbsp sesame oil
- Two tablespoon soy sauce (or tamari for gluten-free)
- 1 tbsp rice vinegar
- 1 tbsp grated ginger
- 1 tbsp sesame seeds
- 2 cups mixed salad greens
- 1 cup shredded carrots
- 1/2 cup sliced cucumber
- 1/4 cup chopped green onions

Method of Preparation:

1. Warm up sesame oil in a pan over medium heat. Add tofu cubes and heat until golden and crispy, approximately 5-7 minutes
2. In a small bowl, mix together soy sauce, rice vinegar, ginger, and sesame seeds.
3. Toss the cooked tofu with the sesame ginger dressing.
4. In a large bowl, mix salad greens, shredded carrots, cucumber, and green onions.
5. Add the sesame ginger tofu on top of the salad and it's ready to be enjoyed!

Nutritional Value (per serving):

Calories: 280, Protein: 20g, Fat: 18g, Carbohydrates: 15g, Fiber: 5g, Net, Carbs: 10g

Chapter 10: 30-Day Meal Plan

This meal plan follows a ketogenic diet approach with a variety of options for breakfast, lunch, and dinner, ensuring variety and balance throughout the month.

Day	*Breakfast*	*Lunch*	*Dinner*
Day 1	Bulletproof Coffee (pg. 18)	Bunless Burger Bowl (pg. 27)	Garlic Butter Shrimp Scampi with Zoodles (pg. 37)
Day 2	Avocado with Smoked Salmon Toast (pg. 18)	Buffalo Chicken Salad (pg. 27)	Cheeseburger Salad (pg. 38)
Day 3	Keto Pancakes (pg. 19)	Salmon Salad Lettuce Wraps (pg. 28)	Baked Salmon with Creamy Spinach (pg. 39)
Day 4	Bacon with Eggs (pg. 20)	Avocado Shrimp Ceviche (pg. 29)	Chicken Fajitas (pg. 39)
Day 5	Chia Pudding (pg. 20)	Keto Cobb Salad (pg. 29)	Cauliflower Mac and Cheese (pg. 40)
Day 6	Keto Breakfast Casserole (pg. 21)	Zucchini Noodles with Pesto and Chicken (pg. 30)	Bacon-Wrapped Asparagus (pg. 41)
Day 7	Keto Smoothie (pg. 22)	Cauliflower Rice Stir-Fry (pg. 31)	Sheet Pan Chicken and Veggies (pg. 41)

Day 8	Keto Omelet (pg. 22)	Keto Chili (pg. 31)	Keto Meatballs with Marinara Sauce (pg. 42)
Day 9	Bulletproof Matcha Latte (pg. 23)	Tuna Salad Stuffed Avocado (pg. 32)	Steak with Roasted Garlic Cauliflower Mash (pg. 42)
Day 10	Keto Yogurt Parfait (pg. 23)	Keto Pizza Chaffles (pg. 33)	One-Pan Baked Chicken Parmesan (pg. 43)
Day 11	Keto Breakfast Burrito (pg. 24)	Chicken Fajita Salad (pg. 33)	Philly Cheesesteak Stuffed Peppers (pg. 44)
Day 12	Keto Egg Muffins (pg. 24)	Egg Salad Lettuce Wraps (pg. 34)	Keto Egg Roll in a Bowl (pg. 44)
Day 13	Cloud Eggs (pg. 25)	Steak Salad with Blue Cheese Dressing (pg. 35)	Grilled Salmon with Avocado Salsa (pg. 45)
Day 14	Keto Granola (pg. 25)	Keto BLT Wraps (pg. 35)	Buffalo Chicken Casserole (pg. 46)

Day 15	Keto Chaffles (pg. 26)	Broccoli and Cheese Soup (pg. 36)	Keto Lemon Garlic Butter Chicken Thighs (pg. 47)
Day 16	Bulletproof Coffee (pg. 18)	Bunless Burger Bowl (pg. 27)	Buffalo Chicken Wings (pg. 47)
Day 17	Avocado with Smoked Salmon Toast (pg. 18)	Buffalo Chicken Salad (pg. 27)	Creamy Spinach-Stuffed Chicken Breast (pg. 48)
Day 18	Keto Pancakes (pg. 19)	Salmon Salad Lettuce Wraps (pg. 28)	Chicken Alfredo Zucchini Noodles (pg. 49)
Day 19	Bacon with Eggs (pg. 20)	Avocado Shrimp Ceviche (pg. 29)	Baked Pesto Chicken with Mozzarella (pg. 49)
Day 20	Chia Pudding (pg. 20)	Keto Cobb Salad (pg. 29)	Keto Chicken Cordon Bleu (pg. 50)
Day 21	Keto Breakfast Casserole (pg. 21)	Zucchini Noodles with Pesto and Chicken (pg. 30)	Jalapeño Popper Chicken Casserole (pg. 51)

Day 22	Keto Smoothie (pg. 22)	Cauliflower Rice Stir-Fry (pg. 31)	Lemon Herb Roasted Chicken (pg. 51)
Day 23	Keto Omelet (pg. 22)	Keto Chili (pg. 31)	Keto Chicken Fajita Bowl (pg. 52)
Day 24	Bulletproof Matcha Latte (pg. 23)	Tuna Salad Stuffed Avocado (pg. 32)	Bacon-Wrapped Chicken Breast (pg. 53)
Day 25	Keto Yogurt Parfait (pg. 23)	Keto Pizza Chaffles (pg. 33)	Keto Chicken Piccata (pg. 53)
Day 26	Keto Breakfast Burrito (pg. 24)	Chicken Fajita Salad (pg. 33)	Thai Coconut Curry Chicken (pg. 54)
Day 27	Keto Egg Muffins (pg. 24)	Egg Salad Lettuce Wraps (pg. 34)	Keto Chicken Tenders (pg. 55)
Day 28	Cloud Eggs (pg. 25)	Steak Salad with Blue Cheese Dressing (pg. 35)	Tuscan Garlic Chicken (pg. 55)
Day 29	Keto Granola (pg. 25)	Keto BLT Wraps (pg. 35)	Chicken Bacon Ranch Skillet (pg. 56)
Day 30	Keto Chaffles (pg. 26)	Broccoli and Cheese Soup (pg. 36)	Garlic Butter Shrimp (pg. 57)

Shopping List

Shopping list based on the 30-day meal plan:

Protein:

Ground beef (80/20 blend or leaner)

Boneless, skinless chicken breasts

Chicken thighs

Steak (for grilling)

Shrimp (peeled and deveined)

Salmon (fresh or canned)

Bacon (uncured)

Eggs (large)

Tuna (canned in water)

Sausage (keto-friendly)

Buffalo chicken wings

Deli meats (sugar-free)

Cheese (mozzarella, cheddar, blue cheese, Parmesan, etc.)

Seafood:

Cod

Crab meat (for crab cakes)

Scallops

Halibut

Mussels

Dairy:

Full-fat Greek yogurt (unsweetened)

Butter (grass-fed)

Ghee

Heavy cream

Cream cheese

Mozzarella

Cheddar

Parmesan

Blue cheese

Vegetables:

Avocados

Zucchini (for noodles)

Bell peppers (variety of colors)

Spinach (fresh or frozen)

Cauliflower (head or pre-riced)

Mushrooms (portobello or white)

Lettuce (romaine, iceberg, or butter)

Broccoli (florets)

Asparagus

Onions (red, white, or yellow)

Garlic (whole or minced)

Tomatoes (canned and fresh)

Green onions

Jalapeño peppers

Celery

Cucumber

Cilantro

Fresh herbs (basil, dill)

Fruits:

Lemons

Limes

Berries (strawberries, blueberries, raspberries)

Coconut (unsweetened flakes)

Nuts and Seeds:

Almonds

Walnuts

Pecans

Chia seeds

Pumpkin seeds

Flaxseeds

Pine nuts

Almond flour

Coconut flour

Condiments & Oils:

Olive oil (extra virgin)

Coconut oil (unrefined)

MCT oil

Apple cider vinegar

Sugar-free ketchup

Dijon mustard

Salsa (sugar-free)

Mayo (keto-friendly)

Soy sauce (or coconut aminos)

Hot sauce (buffalo sauce)

Tomato paste

Coconut milk (unsweetened)

Pesto sauce

Spices and Seasonings:

Salt (Himalayan or sea salt)

Black pepper

Chili powder

Cumin

Paprika

Garlic powder

Onion powder

Italian seasoning

Red pepper flakes

Cinnamon

Sweetener (stevia, monk fruit, etc.)

This shopping list will support the recipes in the 30-day hyper ketosis meal plan with necessary proteins, vegetables, and other pantry staples

Made in United States
Cleveland, OH
27 June 2025

18049479R00050